MW01622826

THE LOVE OF LEARNING

THE LOVE OF LEARNING

Seven Dialogues on the Liberal Arts

Margarita A. Mooney
Editor and Principal Author

CONTRIBUTORS

Robert P. George, *Princeton University*
William Damon, *Stanford University*
Elizabeth Corey, *Baylor University*
Timothy P. O'Malley, *University of Notre Dame*
Carlo Lancellotti, *City University of New York–Staten Island*
George Harne, *University of St. Thomas–Houston*
Roosevelt Montás, *Columbia University*

CLUNY
Providence, Rhode Island

Words of Praise for THE LOVE OF LEARNING *from Scholars and Leaders*

"The impediments to a liberating education in our day and age are many, but Margarita Mooney has recast our challenges as tremendous opportunities for a revival of a genuinely humanizing education. *The Love of Learning* is not merely a case for restoration; it is a deeply enriching exemplification of what such a restoration looks like. Through engaging dialogue and serious and civil reflections on timely and timeless questions, Mooney and her impressive collection of collaborators provide a rich and lasting feast for those involved already in the work of reviving liberal education, as well as an appealing invitation for all others to join us in such efforts."

JONATHAN J. SANFORD,
President and Professor of Philosophy, University of Dallas

"As a long-time advocate and practitioner of liberal arts education, I believe that liberal learning is in essence about cultivating a conversation with the Great Books and with other learners. Presented as a series of pedagogical dialogues between scholars, this book is not merely a conversation *about* the liberal arts, it exemplifies the liberal arts *as* conversation. The book also exemplifies that one can never exhaust the list of great books—I ordered several new books I learned about from these dialogues. The book's study questions and guides for further reading will be useful to students and educators at all levels as well as life-long learners of many backgrounds."

JAMES BERNARD MURPHY,
Professor of Government, Dartmouth College

"Margarita Mooney has given readers a great gift in this series of dialogues. They have the potential to stir a new or renewed desire for learning, give sage counsel about pursuing a liberal education (no matter whether one is in school or not), and model the sorts of conversations that ideally are both a part and a fruit of such an education. Moreover, the book is not just a dialogue between Mooney and her interlocuters or between the reader and the contributors; the volume magnanimously engages with thinkers and theories that stand against the liberal arts tradition, taking them seriously in a refreshing manner that allows for frank rejection of errors without rancor and assimilation of insights with gratitude."

BENJAMIN V. BEIER,
Associate Professor of Education, Hillsdale College

"In response to our polarized era, Margarita Mooney leads us through a series of foundational debates about the human condition, which frame the importance of a liberal arts education in new ways. To be clear, these are debates, and the civil, erudite discussions outlined in *The Love of Learning* provide us with the comforting sense that we can, indeed, deliberate these issues intelligently and in good faith."

PETE PETERSON,
Dean, School of Public Policy, Pepperdine University

"Two of the most important things in life are never ceasing to learn and finding out how to pass on to others the most important things you've learned. Through highly engaging dialogues with some of our age's best teachers, Margarita Mooney's new book inspires and informs us how to do both with enthusiasm and effectiveness."

REV. ROGER J. LANDRY,
Catholic Priest and Author

"A deeply encouraging and accessible book that explains why the liberal arts are vital for genuine education, and why studying them is not only invaluable, but fun!"

ERIC METAXAS, *#1 New York Times bestselling author and host of the nationally syndicated Eric Metaxas Radio Show*

Cluny Media edition, 2021

For more information on Cluny Media and our catalog,
please write to info@clunymedia.com, or to
Cluny Media, P.O. Box 1664, Providence, RI 02901
* VISIT US ONLINE AT WWW.CLUNYMEDIA.COM *

For more information on the Scala Foundation, please visit:
* WWW.SCALAFOUNDATION.ORG *

ISBN: 978-1952826672

Cover design by Clarke & Clarke
Cover image: Pekka Halonen, *Children Reading*,
1916, oil painting
Courtesy of Wikimedia Commons

CONTENTS

ACKNOWLEDGEMENTS

MARGARITA A. MOONEY

THIS BOOK is the result of creativity that emerged from the chaos of the campus shutdowns caused by COVID-19 beginning in March 2020. The seven dialogue partners—Robert P. George, William Damon, Elizabeth Corey, Timothy P. O'Malley, Carlo Lancellotti, George Harne, and Roosevelt Montás—eagerly tuned in from home over Zoom to engage in these friendly, scholarly dialogues with me and an audience across the United States and the globe. The participants in the webinars provided additional questions for the topics we discussed, which were edited to flow into the dialogue between me and each scholar. Two of the contributors—Carlo Lancellotti and Roosevelt Montás—had previously dialogued with me at in-person Scala Foundation events in 2019. Their dialogues in this book include some parts of those conversations as well.

During the 2019–2020 academic year, I was on sabbatical from my teaching at Princeton Theological Seminary and was a Visiting Research Fellow at the Center for the Study of Religion at Princeton University. I am grateful to both institutions for helping me further my scholarship on education during that time.

Michael Paul Cartledge helped me pivot Scala's resources quickly to organize the webinar series that led to this book. His dedication to Scala's vision helped me bring order to Scala's shift to online programming while he dealt with the chaos of moving four times between March and August 2020 with three children and a pregnant wife. Bess Blackburn skillfully edited the videos, placing full-length videos on Scala's YouTube channel, as well as shorter videos on particular questions.

John Emmet Clarke of Cluny Media enthusiastically embraced the vision for this book and provided expert guidance throughout this project. Caitrin Keiper provided outstanding editorial assistance to edit the transcripts for style while maintaining the natural voice of each contributor. Henry Burt also read each chapter carefully and wrote discussion questions for the chapters, along with assistance from Brooke Caton, and also helped me compile the short guides to key texts in educational philosophy. Timothy O'Malley provided assistance with the short guide to John Dewey's writings on education. Brett Bertucio and William Gonch also provided helpful feedback on the book's introduction and conclusion, along with James Bernard Murphy of Dartmouth College and Benjamin Beier of Hillsdale College. The students in the joint Pepperdine–Scala summer program in 2020 were the first to engage with the videos and transcripts in the classroom. Their enthusiasm and questions provided invaluable input to the discussion questions, short guides to key texts, and introduction and conclusion.

The co-sponsors of the webinars included the Portsmouth Institute for Faith and Culture, the McGrath Center for Church Life at the University of Notre Dame, the James Madison Program in American Ideals and Institutions at Princeton University, the Pepperdine School of Public Policy, Catholic Studies at the University of St. Thomas in St. Paul, the Baylor Institute for Faith and Learning, and the Stanford Center on Adolescence. I am profoundly grateful to Christopher Fisher, Timothy O'Malley, Robert George, Pete Peterson, Erika Kidd, Lori Kanitz, and

William Damon for sharing the love of learning through their amazing programs.

None of this could have happened without the benefactors to Scala's programs who supported Scala in the midst of so much uncertainty in 2020. Renzo Canetta provided encouragement and wisdom as I pivoted Scala's programs in a time of much uncertainty. My heartfelt thanks go to the members of the Leadership Circle that supported this work that led to this book: T. J. Rodgers and Valeta Massey, Dr. and Mrs. James Reibel, Tom Kovalcik, Al Furth, Duncan Sahner, Pete Peterson and the Pepperdine School of Public Policy, the Charles and Ann Johnson Family Foundation, the Dian Graves Owen Foundation, the Institute for Humane Studies, and four anonymous donors. Numerous other supporters also contributed financially to this project. Although there are too many to name here, please know that it because of the generous financial support of each and every one of you that these important ideas will now reach thousands more hungry souls seeking truth.

MARGARITA A. MOONEY
Princeton, New Jersey
March 1, 2021

INTRODUCTION

MARGARITA A. MOONEY

HUMANS HAVE an insatiable desire for meaning and for knowledge. This desire does not disappear when we leave a particular classroom or finish entirely our formal schooling. Every stage of life is another part of the journey of learning, one which continuously deepens our sense of meaning. This book, through a series of dialogues between me and seven scholars and practitioners of the liberal arts tradition of education, encourages readers to ask the fundamental questions about why humans thirst for knowledge and how that knowledge is connected to serving others and loving God.

In these dialogues, we engage with European scholars in the Catholic intellectual tradition such as Jacques Maritain, John Henry Newman, and Luigi Giussani, whose integral humanist approach to education contrasts with the problem-solving approach of the Brazilian Paulo Freire and the American John Dewey, both of whom neglect the human desire for contemplative truth. As a liberal arts education is both contemplative *and* practical, these dialogues also engage with practical problems such as the loss of attention and the forms of student activism that undermine truth-seeking—problems so well captured by scholars like Neal Postman, Greg Lukianoff, and Jonathan Haidt.

Educational institutions are under tremendous pressure today to demonstrate their relevance for one or another economic or political end. In the nearly three decades I have been either a student or a professor in higher education, I have seen students become increasingly focused on the instrumental gains from their education. Without discounting the importance of the practical skills or social goals of education, the liberal arts tradition upholds the idea that education ought to be disinterested and useful at the same time but in different respects.

In recent decades in the United States, all levels of education, from K–12 to higher education, have seen some renewed interest in classical liberal arts models of education, including experiences of beauty as part of coming to know objective truth. The intellectual virtues required not only to learn from past traditions of knowledge but also to exercise the open-mindedness and curiosity that lead to new knowledge demand a holistic approach to educational curricula, educational settings, and teacher-student interactions. Education should not seek to produce quasi-robots who have lost the desire for connecting the material world with the sublime. A good education reveals to students how things work and also guides them to perceive the beauty behind all things.

These dialogues illustrate how, across a variety of disciplines and a variety of institutional types, education can be connected to exploring the foundational questions about our humanity. An account of what the liberal arts tradition of education is, and how it differs from a purely pragmatic or technical view of education, emerges out of these dialogues as they explore the key ideas that have shaped debates in American educational institutions.

The order of the chapters moves from discussing the philosophical roots of how education has been understood and practiced in the United States to creative ways of teaching in the liberal arts tradition. In Chapter 1,

I discuss with Princeton University Professor of Jurisprudence Robert P. George his journey from childhood in West Virginia to the elite college classrooms where he learned to ask *why* things are as they are, not just how things work. We explore the importance of tradition in education, along with a lesson Professor George learned from his mother and best teachers: think for yourself.

In Chapter 2, I explore with Stanford University Professor of Education William Damon how his early experiences with moral exemplars in impoverished communities led him to conduct psychology research on moral education in order to develop a vision for integral, transformative education.

In my dialogue with Professor Elizabeth Corey of the Politics Department and Honors College at Baylor University, Chapter 3 explores Professor Corey's early love of music and how that led her to fall in love with the holistic foundations of a liberal arts education. In her teaching, she leads students beyond achievement culture so they can form authentic friendships, pursue the truth in community, and fall in love with learning again.

Timothy P. O'Malley, Director of Education at the McGrath Institute for Church Life at the University of Notre Dame, explores with me in Chapter 4 his own discovery of the contemplative aspect of experiential education. Experiential education at its best is fully personal—one's immersion in the world can be the doorway to transcendence and lived tradition.

Chapter 5 is a dialogue between me and Carlo Lancellotti, Mathematical Physicist at the City University of New York in Staten Island. Coming of age during the student protests in Italy in the 1960s, Professor Lancellotti discusses with me how his encounter with the Benedictine tradition allowed him to discover the beautiful, awe-inspiring aspects of scientific inquiry. As a practicing scientist, he shares with students the presence of poetic truth in the material world.

George Harne, former President of Magdalen College of the Liberal Arts, talks with me in Chapter 6 how his love and talent for music led him to become the first in his family to attend college. This love led him to incorporate the fine arts and questions of beauty into a holistic educational curriculum that unites science, experiential learning, and worship––education that has the capacity to transform all kinds of students.

Chapter 7 is a dialogue between me and Professor Roosevelt Montás, the former director of Columbia University's Core Curriculum and Senior Lecturer in American Studies and English at Columbia. Professor Montás shares with me how, as a teenage immigrant to New York City from the Dominican Republic, he learned that the Great Books transcend particular experiences and speak to fundamental human questions. His teaching continues to unite students from different backgrounds in a common journey of truth-seeking.

Across each of the chapters, I share bits of my own story as a Cuban American woman seeking to integrate my love of learning with my Catholic faith. Each chapter guides readers to continue their own lifelong learning by suggesting readings from key texts from authors old and new, from Plato, Aristotle and Augustine, to John Henry Newman, Jacques Maritain and Luigi Giussani. I conclude with numerous practical suggestions on pursuing a liberal arts education at any stage in life, including a guide for discussion groups, and points readers toward numerous popular publications which connect the love of learning to our contemporary culture.

❋ ❋ ❋

These conversations, both in content and in format, aim to move past the stereotype that liberal arts education is for the elite. Any purposeful human life must consider and respond to the fundamental question of who we are as humans and ask how we are meant to develop our talents through education. Liberal arts education is key to social order, not just because of the inclusion of great texts that have shaped civilization (although that is important) but because a liberal arts education has a holistic view of the person. In particular, the liberal arts tradition is holistic in its acknowledgment that experiences of beauty shape our capacity for attention to all of reality. Our capacity to be attentive to beauty is at risk of being diminished through the dispersion of mental energy that leads to inner fragmentation and student burnout. A mind open to God, to mystery, to wonder, is not the opposite of scientific reason, but is integral to comprehending the full significance of reality and recovering the love of learning.

At the time I hosted the webinars on which this book is based, March 2020 to June 2020, the United States was in the first few months of the COVID-19 pandemic. Educational practices rapidly moved online for many people, including myself and the other contributors to this book. But even as K–12 schools and college campuses have gradually re-opened, many more parents are actively educating their children, and themselves, at home. Many more students are finding creative ways to form communities of learners.

This book emerged out of the work of Scala Foundation, which I started in 2016. Scala aims to extend the vision of liberal arts education by organizing student reading groups, faculty seminars, intensive summer programs, conferences, and webinars that examine the intellectual trends that have shaped educational culture and practices. I started Scala because I believe renewing a transformative, holistic liberal arts education is essential for students and teachers in their personal development and for the common good. Inspired by a vision of education grounded in the conviction that human beings are created in the image of God, educating the whole person can never be likened to a scientific or social experiment. Each person is unique, irreplaceable, and has an inherent dignity and personal vocation. Education needs to create an environment that models a view of leisure and friendship as intrinsic human goods that inspire a life-long love of learning and the pursuit of truth and beauty in community.

Although students and educators may take a special interest in this book, the main ideas of this book should matter to everyone because education is crucial to integral human formation. The true end of education is forming the whole person to seek the truth with passion and desire. Anyone who cares about living a meaningful life will come to see that these foundational questions about education are really about what it means to live a life that unites knowledge and passion to help one grow in wisdom and purpose.

Regardless of your own educational background or occupation, this book will show you how to be both a learner and an educator in any circumstance. These dialogues will challenge you to think about the personal habits and communities we all need to help us in this life-long quest for liberal learning, which is the only kind of education adequate for people whose lives are characterized by a love of freedom and deep sense of purpose.

Many of the ideas discussed in each of the chapters are grounded in a Judeo-Christian view of the person as created for greatness, but also fallen in sin and in need of redemption. But not all contributors in this volume are uniform in their view of religion or the transcendent. The point of agreement among the contributors to this volume is that the relationship between faith and reason should not be deemed beyond the realm of rational, scholarly discussion. All of the contributors believe that education should lead people to the truth—a point that people of any faith or of no particular faith tradition can agree upon.

In order to encourage readers to engage in a deep internal dialogue with each chapter and discuss what they are learning with others, each chapter contains suggested questions for discussion. These questions are meant to help readers ponder important concepts, think through key statements, and provoke thoughts about how the lessons of each chapter may (or may not) apply in various contexts. Each chapter also contains a list of references discussed in the dialogue, as well as additional suggested readings for further and deeper exploration of the ideas covered in each chapter. I have also included guidelines for those who wish to read this book as part of a class, reading group or church group, or among fellow educators, parents, or students, and I have written short guides to books by seven authors discussed across several of the chapters as well. These guides provide an overview of the key questions and debates in educational philosophy and practice.

I sincerely hope that this book rekindles your passion to learn so you never stop asking questions and seeking answers!

IN BRIEF, this volume contributes to understanding the importance of liberal arts education, by addressing topics or arguments such as:

- How to get past the stereotype that liberal arts education is for the elite. Standards of excellence in education should be for everyone.

- How to challenge the false dichotomy between liberal arts education and a useful or technical education. Only a good education can be useful, and liberal arts education aids a practical education in many ways.
- The false opposition between beauty and reason. Experiences of beauty shape our capacity for attention to all of reality. Beauty leads us to the truth. Our capacity to enter into beauty is at risk of being dumbed down through the dispersion of mental energy that leads to inner fragmentation. A reason open to God, to mystery, to wonder, is not the opposite of scientific reason, but integral to it.
- Liberal education is key to social order, not just because of the inclusion of great texts that have shaped civilization (although that is important) but because a liberal arts education treats the person holistically.
- One need not have a liberal arts education or teach in a school dedicated to liberal arts to live out these ideals. Anyone can be an exemplary educator who transforms students' lives because anyone dedicated to the life-long pursuit of knowledge is educating oneself and has the capacity to educate others.

REFERENCES

Dewey, John. *Democracy and Education: An Introduction to the Philosophy of Education*. New York: Macmillan, 1921.

Freire, Paulo. *Pedagogy of the Oppressed*. New York: Bloomsbury Academic, 2018.

Giussani, Luigi. *The Risk of Education: Discovering Our Ultimate Destiny*. Montreal: McGill-Queen's University Press, 2019.

Lukianoff, Greg, and Jonathan Haidt. *The Coddling of the American Mind: How Good Intentions and Bad Ideas Are Setting Up a Generation for Failure*. New York: Penguin Books, 2019.

Maritain, Jacques. *Education at the Crossroads*. New Haven: Yale University Press, 1960.

Postman, Neil. *Amusing Ourselves to Death: Public Discourse in an Age of Show Business*. New York: Penguin Books, 2005.

THE LOVE OF LEARNING

ROBERT P. GEORGE is McCormick Professor of Jurisprudence and Director of the James Madison Program in American Ideals and Institutions at Princeton University. In addition to his academic service, Professor George has served as Chairman of the U.S. Commission on International Religious Freedom. He has also served on the President's Council on Bioethics, the United States Commission on Civil Rights, and as the U.S. member of UNESCO's World Commission on the Ethics of Science and Technology. Professor George is author and editor of numerous books and scholarly articles, including *The Clash of Orthodoxies*, *Great Cases in Constitutional Law*, and *The Cambridge Companion to Natural Law*. He has also written for *The New York Times*, *The Wall Street Journal*, *The Washington Post*, *First Things*, the *Boston Review*, and the *Times Literary Supplement*. A graduate of Swarthmore College, Professor George holds M.T.S. and J.D. degrees from Harvard University and the degrees of D.Phil., B.C.L., D.C.L., and D.Litt. from Oxford University. He holds twenty-two honorary degrees and has received numerous awards including Princeton University's President's Award for Distinguished Teaching.

CHAPTER 1

Does Human Nature Matter for Education?

ROBERT P. GEORGE *and* MARGARITA A. MOONEY

MOONEY: How did your education take shape? Who were your influences?

GEORGE: I grew up in West Virginia, where I had something of a Huck Finn boyhood, hunting and fishing and playing bluegrass music. Both of my grandfathers were immigrant coal miners. My mother's father came from Calabria in southern Italy, fleeing abject poverty. My father's father came from Syria, fleeing Ottoman oppression. They ended up in Appalachia, where they worked in the mines and on the railroads. After a while, my maternal grandfather was able to save up enough money to establish a little grocery business.

Neither of my parents went to college, but both highly valued education in the way that immigrant families often do. They preached it to my four brothers and me as a way to move up in the world—to grow in knowledge, specifically the sort of practical and professional knowledge that would lead to a professional career and higher social standing.

I thought that was what education was. And there's a lot of truth in that, but there's also more to it. It was only later that I began to learn that the pursuit of knowledge is something valuable for its own sake. That realization put me on the path to my vocation of scholarship and teaching.

Growing up, my brothers and I attended public and Catholic parochial schools. When it came time to go to college, my parents—especially my mother—strongly felt that we should go to the best college we could find. My mother wanted us to go out of state. She didn't know much about it, but her sense was that there were superior colleges elsewhere and that we should aspire to attend them.

My parents took me to visit Swarthmore College and I fell in love with it. I was struck by the intellectual intensity of the discussions even though I wasn't on track at that time to be a scholar. Fortunately, I was admitted. I struggled during my freshman year because I was so far behind my classmates in terms of training, but I had help from a couple of wonderful professors who took me under their wings.

I was then able then to catch up and succeed academically, which enabled me to go on to Harvard for a law degree and a master's degree. By that point, I had come to a fundamentally different understanding of education, a deep appreciation of the pursuit of knowledge as an end in itself. The field I was most interested in was at the nexus of philosophy of law and moral and political philosophy. The best place to study that was Oxford University, where I had the opportunity to learn from two giants of the field, Joseph Raz and John Finnis.

After graduate school, I came to teach at Princeton, where I have been ever since. In 1993 I published *Making Men Moral: Civil Liberties and Public Morality,* which challenged the dominant thinking in contemporary political theory that "private" virtue has no place, or only a narrow and restricted place, in discussions of the public good.

Mooney: In *Education at the Crossroads* (1942), French philosopher Jacques Maritain says that the true end of education is to form the conscience of the person to seek the truth. What happened to convince you of this?

George: It was *the* transformative event in my adult life. It happened in a college course—a pretty straightforward and not especially remarkable introductory survey course in political philosophy. When we read the first assignment from Plato's dialogues, the *Gorgias,* suddenly I was forced to consider a question that had never occurred to me before: Why do we pursue knowledge?

In Plato's dialogues, Socrates is the hero debating with his interlocutors, the Sophists. The Sophists were accomplished rhetoric and debate teachers, something like law professors. The families of privileged young Athenian men paid money to the Sophists for this training to learn how to make impressive arguments, present themselves in the public square, and become important and influential. To the Sophists, discussion, debate, and dialogue were the means to such ends and that's how they defended them.

Socrates, as Plato presents him to us, questions all of that. What's really important, he says, is knowledge for its own sake. The dedication to truth is inherently enriching and makes for a fulfilling life.

I'd never considered the question, much less got the right answer. Look, there's no doubt that knowledge is instrumentally valuable. By pursuing knowledge, we cure diseases. We build buildings. We create great works of art and literature. Culture itself is the fruit of knowledge. All of this holds great instrumental value.

Wealth, status, influence, prestige, and power are things that matter too; they can be used for good ends. I don't discourage my students from pursuing them. But they're means, not ends. Ends are things like friendship, knowledge, virtue, faith in God, beauty.

Mooney: When we marvel at *how* something works, that is the beginning of scientific inquiry. When we ask ourselves *why*, it is a moral question. When education focuses solely on the *how* questions, students aren't being given the chance to ask these *why* questions. If we're not educating the moral, the intuitive, the emotional, the longing for beauty, then we've left out a key part of who we are.

People don't often want to talk about who we are as human beings. They just want to get on to the practical things. But the most fundamental questions are about our human good, and if we can't answer those questions, we're going to get the downstream social and political questions really wrong. Why is it so hard to have a dialogue about who we are as human beings?

George: There are different impediments for different people. Some people have adopted a pragmatist approach to life: there's no point in speculating about questions that aren't of immediate practical significance. My response to them is that these questions are in a certain sense the *most* practical questions to ask because there's no point in choosing one course of action over another unless you know at some level why you are doing it. Sometimes, very important life choices depend on where we come down on the great existential questions of meaning and value.

For some people, the impediment is that they're ideologically locked into the idea that these questions do not have answers. That in itself becomes their dogma. They often claim not to be anti-dogmatists, and to object to religion because it's dogmatic. Someone who's not dogmatic will not begin with any such assumption but will just try to begin thinking through those questions, seeing where reflection leads when drawing on the best that's been thought and said.

Now, it might be that your conclusion ultimately is there are no answers to these questions. I personally don't think that's right. But even if that's your conclusion, you shouldn't start with that as your premise. You need to reason your way to that conclusion and have reasons for drawing it.

Mooney: Even to ask these questions assumes a conscience, an inner life. There is a misconception that who we are is determined by outside forces such as social roles, political circumstances, or material conditions. Maritain's project is to rescue the inner dimension of the human person from this erasure. To be sure, the social or political or material contexts may be strong influences, but Maritain insists that there is an inner core of the person, the soul, that is free.

Many secular universities prefer a Rawlsian veil of ignorance—where our ultimate faith commitments are excluded from public reasoning. That has led to an assumption that to talk about one's ultimate commitments is to impose them on others. But I've seen a shift in younger generations who want to hear authentic answers to these questions about life—from a variety of perspectives, including from various faith traditions.

But some views of education prevalent today focus more on forming one's political views rather than on forming one's conscience. The two are related, but they should not be equated. For example, Paulo Freire's 1968 book *Pedagogy of the Oppressed* is one of the best-selling books on education of all time. What seems to resonate with people is Freire's emphasis on dialogue between teachers and students, breaking down what he calls the banking model of education in which students are receptacles into which teachers make deposits of information. He says that what education should be is a dialogue, an encounter between your own personal experience and what you are learning in school. This view of education is appealing to many because it brings the personal identity of the student into the classroom.

But Freire makes a lot of *a priori* philosophical assumptions. His views of education are based on the Marxist class analysis that there are two kinds of people, the oppressed and the oppressors. The purpose of education for Freire is to form people's consciousness of their historical role in order to bring about a particular political goal—the end of political oppression.

Jacques Maritain's book *Education at the Crossroads* appeared well before *Pedagogy of the Oppressed*, but it anticipates the themes that Freire deals with. In Maritain's short, powerful book on education, he critiques the dominant paradigms of education that he saw in the United States in the 1940s. Those two dominant paradigms are pragmatism, often associated with John Dewey's views on education, and philosophical Marxism, which is clearly the basis of Freire's view of education.

In *Education at the Crossroads*, Maritain says that we can't understand the end of education if we don't ponder the meaning of the human person as not merely a physical being but created for knowledge and love as ends in an of themselves. Education has to first and foremost form the inner dynamism of the student.

For Maritain, that inner dynamism includes the relationship between the person and the creator, not just the relationship between the person and his or her place in history or the social order. Maritain warns that concerns about political problems, as important as those concerns may be, cannot overtake the formation of the inner conscience of the person. Forming the conscience of the student is very challenging and can't be reduced to educating people about politics.

If the inner life of a person is nothing more than an expression of a social context or historical dialectic, then we end up with a dumbed-down pragmatism or a soft totalitarianism in education that simply tells everybody what to think and how to act. If we eradicate the mystery of the human person as the heart of education, we quickly lose the intrinsic goods of community, love, friendship, and solidarity. If reason and the passions are separated, I fear that some students may find radical ideological political projects attractive precisely because they claim to unite reasons and emotions, becoming a kind of religion.

Speaking as a Catholic (though this viewpoint is held by many others), I believe we're endowed with a certain nature by our creator. We're free because our creator made us to become free.

George: According to the biblical story, we human beings are made in the very image and likeness of God. We are also made from the very dust of the earth. We're very low and very high at the same time; we can all find both extremes within our own experience.

The line between good and evil, as Aleksander Solzhenitsyn said, is drawn through every human heart. Being cognizant of that should keep us humble. It should also inspire and motivate us to be the best we possibly can—after all, we're made in the image and likeness of God.

As dust of the earth, we have our limitations. We are flesh and blood. We have emotions as well as reason. We have passion as well as rationality. And passion can mislead us. Therefore some philosophies, such as Buddhism or extreme Stoicism, suggest that passion is to be eliminated. This is not my view.

Plato taught that it's important for passion to be under the control of reason; this is the ordering of the soul that enables human flourishing. But when passion gets the whip hand over reason, not only will we do things that are wrong and destructive for ourselves and others, we will then fabricate rationalizations. We will instrumentalize reason and use it to justify things that at some level we know to be wrong.

Our faculties of freedom and reason are what make us Godlike. Here I'm drawing on an insight from Thomas Aquinas and the Jewish and Christian tradition that informed him. God is able to envision a state of affairs that doesn't yet exist, recognize the value of bringing that state of affairs into being, and then act freely on the basis of his understanding to do so. God is not pushed around by instinct or impulse.

We share this ability, to a point. We are animals, with instincts, impulses, emotions, passions; we're limited in our Godlikeness. But in possession of free will and reason, we can deliberate and choose our actions. We're able to transcend the material aspects of ourselves—our animality. Our animality is part of us—I'm not denying it—but what's distinctive and important about us is that we're not merely material or animal. The evidence for that is our experience of our own rationality and freedom.

The implication of our freedom and reason is that we are also responsible. We are under judgment. There are moral norms governing our lives. All of this presupposes that freedom and reason are not illusions.

We are animals, with instincts, impulses, emotions, passions; we're limited in our Godlikeness. But in possession of free will and reason, we can deliberate and choose our actions. We're able to transcend the material aspects of ourselves—our animality.

MOONEY: Insofar as impulses and instincts are part of human nature, do they also reflect God's image? When you talk about reason as our most Godlike feature, how do you see it in relationship to the emotions and the passions in terms of who we are as human beings?

GEORGE: First, we must understand that reason is not a calculating machine. This common but emaciated understanding of reason is a distinctively post-Enlightenment, modern view. But beginning in the 1950s and 1960s, something important happened in philosophy called the neo-Aristotelian revival. This strain of thought recovered Aristotle's much richer idea of reason, especially in the domain of action, what Aristotle calls "practical" as opposed to "theoretical reason"—reasoning about what is worthwhile, what we ought to do, how we ought to conduct ourselves.

The real richness of reason is that it attains truth not by quantification or by calculation, but by comprehending the value of goods such as having or being a friend, pursuing knowledge, developing skills and talents, seeking a relationship with God, understanding and appreciating beauty. These are the things that give us more than merely instrumental reasons for action.

With that view of reason, then we can start thinking about how emotion figures in. As I said, I reject the idea that passion is just bad and that we should get rid of it. We need to get our emotions properly ordered, under the control and direction of reason. But we *should* have a passion for justice. We should have a passion for beauty. We should have a passion for goodness. We should have a passion for doing what's right. It's passion that gets us up out of our chairs to do something. It's one thing to intellectually appreciate the value of an action; it's another thing to get yourself up and motivated, because doing that is often hard work.

We ascribe reason and passion to God. We speak of God's anger or God's pleasure. We're not quite sure what we mean in saying that, because God is certainly not a victim of his emotions. He's not pushed around by them. Strictly speaking, I'd have to say God doesn't have emotions. But they are gesturing toward something—what God loves or what God does not want.

MOONEY: We feel our way to the truth because the truth is attractive. The truth is drawing us in. That's when we can bring together the conceptual, the scientific, and also the poetic aspects of knowledge and integrate them with our interior life. That knowledge becomes unitary. A holistic education is when emotions and passions are integrated with the analytical problem-solving mind.

In *The Risk of Education* (2019), Luigi Giussani suggests that we take these questions about the nature of the human person and open them up for rational debate. To do this, he says, teachers should acknowledge that they're starting this debate from a particular tradition, from a point of view. What would you say is the role of tradition in education?

GEORGE: I've learned a lot from the philosopher Alasdair MacIntyre. In his 1988 book *Whose Justice? Which Rationality?*, MacIntyre explains that there is no neutral vantage point, no Archimedean point from which we assess great existential questions. We're always coming from a standpoint, and we're shaped by traditions of thought—traditions that supply things like language and concepts that enable us to think at all.

Kids are brought up in one tradition or another—secular or religious, philosophical, a set of ideas, or some other worldview. Whatever it may be, that tradition enables the child to begin thinking about questions. He encounters some of the answers that the tradition itself supplies. He may or may not find them satisfactory. Often he begins to notice that the tradition generates questions that it cannot satisfactorily answer. Though the tradition helped open the questions, it does not provide the resources to answer them. MacIntyre says that at this point the tradition goes into an epistemological crisis.

Finding the tradition he's in to be lacking on its own terms, the questioner begins to look for alternatives—for a tradition that's capable of generating and shaping those same questions and can offer more coherent answers. This is how conversions happen.

MacIntyre himself is a person who's been through several conversions. He began as an Irish Protestant, made his way through logical positivism and pseudo-Marxism, and then became a Catholic. He arrives at these observations by reflecting on his own personal journey.

I can say the same for my own experience. I haven't ever been through a religious conversion, but when I had my life-altering encounter with Plato, it made me rethink everything. It's in those experiences of raising questions and looking for the resources to answer them that development and transformations happen, whether it's full conversion or not.

MOONEY: Giussani says tradition is like a backpack: everybody comes into school carrying their books and their pencils in that backpack. Part of what we need to do as educators is to unpack what's in that backpack—that is, the student's tradition. We need to pull it out for rational examination. And doing that is a risk.

GEORGE: Yes, when you're really committed to truth-seeking, you don't know where this inquiry is going to lead. You don't know who you're going to be at the end of it—if there ever is an end of it. Learning is a lifelong business.

You take a certain existential risk in doing that because we human beings tend to wrap our emotions rather tightly around our convictions. We're afraid of being forced to change them by the power of reason or the logic of the thing or the evidence that's presented. You take a risk when you open yourself up to truth.

A good education is unsettling. As a teacher, it is my job to unsettle my students and get them into the truth-seeking mode.

MOONEY: What do you do if you're in an institution where students aren't encouraged to be asking these questions? How do you bring this into the classroom?

A good education is unsettling. As a teacher, it is my job to unsettle my students and get them into the truth-seeking mode.

GEORGE: Speaking from my undergraduate experience, my advice is this: there will be one or two or three professors there who are interested in these questions, believe me. They're thinkers and truth-seekers, and they want you to be one. Seek them out. Ask around about the different professors. Even from your peers, you'll be able to figure out who they are.

You don't have to get aggressive and push your own answers to the questions. Just ask them. If you've got a view, you might put it on the table and say, "Here's how I think about it. I'm curious how other people think about it." Who is going to think of you as stuck up or arrogant?

MOONEY: You have to have a sense of where your peers or friends or teachers are in this journey, too. Don't expect that every dialogue is going to end in perfect agreement. Be open-ended and seek out people similar to and different from you. You'll find both.

When students encounter a dialogue in which the conclusions are not already given, they are excited. The questions are truly open. The professors and the students are on this journey together. A good educator has a moral responsibility to travel with students to put their own understanding back together. Giussani says that an educator must open up these big questions and be willing to accompany students in finding answers.

GEORGE: My mother used to say to me, "Always think for yourself." In other words, you're responsible for your own opinions and beliefs and choices and actions. You can't rely on, or permit, other people to do your thinking for you. We need to encourage our students to do more independent thinking. Don't just pick up your ideas from the ambient culture. Don't just go along with whatever the trendy thing is. Think for yourself. It's a hard job. It's difficult, and it's risky. But you're responsible for doing it.

DISCUSSION QUESTIONS

1. George states, "A holistic education is when emotions and their passions are integrated with the analytical problem-solving mind." What sort of emotions do you "trust" when deciding whether or not to allow yourself to pursue a certain passion? What are some factors outside of your emotions that help you make this decision? On the other hand, are there any emotions that you are distrustful of? Again, what are some contextual factors that account for your distrust?

2. Name a time when the questions you contemplated could not be adequately addressed by your worldview. How did you respond? What resources did you seek out? Did you alter your worldview?

3. George states, "We're afraid of being forced to change them [our beliefs] by the power of reason or the logic of the thing or the evidence

that's presented. You take a risk when you open yourself up to truth." In this day and age, what sort of truths does society seem hesitant to open itself up to? Are there truths that you personally are afraid to examine, for fear of the change or conviction that they might bring? What are the ramifications of protecting oneself from examining the truth? How about on a societal level?

4. Do you think education should be used to promote a particular political project or type of social change? Why or why not?

5. George emphasizes the importance of thinking for yourself, forming your own judgments of things based on reason and evidence. Can you think of a time when you adopted a viewpoint just because you heard it repeated but upon reflection realized you didn't agree? Is it always possible to think through for ourselves, independently, every value and judgment we hold?

6. George states: "Our faculties of freedom and reason are what make us Godlike. Here I'm drawing on an insight from Thomas Aquinas and the Jewish and Christian tradition that informed him... We are animals, with instincts, impulses, emotions, passions; we're limited in our Godlikeness. But in possession of free will and reason, we can deliberate and choose our actions. We're able to transcend the material aspects of ourselves—our animality... The implication of our freedom and reason is that we are also responsible. We are under judgment. There are moral norms governing our lives." Do you agree with his depiction of human nature? Is this description of human nature valid even for people who may not come from the Jewish or Christian tradition he says undergirds this conviction?

REFERENCES

Aristotle. *The Nicomachean Ethics*. Translated by David Ross. Oxford: Oxford University Press, 2009.

Freire, Paulo. *Pedagogy of the Oppressed*. New York: Bloomsbury Academic, 2018.

George, Robert P. *Making Men Moral: Civil Liberties and Public Morality*. Oxford: Clarendon Press, 1995.

Giussani, Luigi. *The Risk of Education: Discovering Our Ultimate Destiny*. Montreal: McGill-Queen's University Press, 2019.

MacIntyre, Alasdair. *Whose Justice? Which Rationality?* Notre Dame: University of Notre Dame Press, 1988.

Maritain, Jacques. *Education at the Crossroads*. New Haven: Yale University Press, 1960.

Plato. *Gorgias*. Translated by Donald Zeyl. Indianapolis: Hackett Publishing Company, Inc., 1987.

Solzhenitsyn, Aleksandr. *The Gulag Archipelago*. London: Random House, 2003.

ADDITIONAL READINGS

Blum, Christopher, and Joshua Hochschild. *A Mind at Peace: Reclaiming an Ordered Soul in the Age of Distraction*. Manchester: Sophia Institute Press, 2017.

Mooney, Margarita. "Educating the Human Person." *Real Clear Policy*, October 4, 2019, at www.realclearpolicy.com/articles/2019/10/04/educating_the_human_person_111282.html.

≈

WILLIAM DAMON is Professor of Education at Stanford University, Director of the Stanford Center on Adolescence, and Senior Fellow, by courtesy, at the Hoover Institution. He is one of the world's leading researchers on the development of purpose. He is the author of *The Path to Purpose*. Damon's other books include *The Moral Child*; *Greater Expectations* (winner of the Parent's Choice Book Award); *Some Do Care: Lives of Moral Commitment* (with Anne Colby); *Good Work* (with Howard Gardner and Mihaly Csikszentmihalyi); and *The Power of Ideals: The Real Story of Moral Choice* (also with Anne Colby). Damon's ongoing work includes studying the development of purpose in the college years and studying family purposes across generations. Damon has been elected to membership in the National Academy of Education and the American Academy of Arts and Sciences.

CHAPTER 2

Every Child Has a Spark: The Tandem of Internal Motivation and Co-Learning

William Damon *and* Margarita A. Mooney

Mooney: Bill, where did you go to school when you were young? What about your own educational experiences led you to develop such a rich research agenda? How have you applied those insights to your research on education?

Damon: The professional part of my education was pretty traditional. I went to Harvard University and studied social psychology there, and then to the University of California at Berkeley, where I studied developmental psychology.

I had very good academic training in those disciplines, but a couple of stories about less formal parts of my education played a big role in why I got interested in moral and social processes, which eventually led to my studies of purpose and moral commitment. I'll tell you one very early story, and one very late, in my education.

The early one was in the ninth grade. I had little use for school at that age, and I was basically a lazy, unengaged student. However, I did get involved in one thing that interested me, which was my school newspaper. I covered sports, which I loved at the time.

One of my earliest stories for the newspaper was a game assigned to me for our junior varsity soccer team. Our team played a group of Hungarian kids, immigrants who had formed a little get-together team. They played much better than our junior varsity team because they came from Europe, and nobody was playing soccer in the U.S. at the time.

I hung around afterwards and spoke to the Hungarian kids. They had recently come over, having escaped communism, and were so thrilled about being in America. They had nothing. Their parents had packed them green pepper and bacon fat sandwiches. I was feeling sorry for these kids, but they were so happy, and they talked about what a pleasure it was to be in a free society, and to have opportunities.

That was the story I wrote for the school newspaper—not the story about the game. I had found out something new that I knew nothing about—I learned about the process of immigration, and I had the sense that I had never appreciated the special parts of growing up in America. Then I discovered that my friends read the piece and were really interested in it—that other people enjoyed and learned from my writing.

That was how the seeds of my academic interests were planted. I decided to learn how to be a better writer and how to do research. I really trace my own purpose in life back to that newspaper experience. It wasn't a class or a teacher—it was that extracurricular activity that was educative for me because it motivated me to then take my schoolwork seriously.

My later story of educational formation happened after I was already doing psychological research and working in developmental psychology. I was a professor at this point, and I got involved in a project with my wife, Anne Colby, on studying American moral exemplars. These were people who had dedicated decades of their life to things like charity, world peace, and environmental causes.

I'll never forget the time I spent with one of them named Suzie Valadez. She was living in El Paso, Texas, and she would cross the border every day to Juarez to work with the children and families who were living around a garbage dump. The kids loved her.

I spent a few fourteen-hour days with this woman, who was in her seventies. I was in my late thirties, and she exhausted me! She was full of joy and spirit, and she was a woman of deep faith.

She had only an eighth-grade education herself, but she had learned how to do everything from building hospitals and starting schools to raising money. I wanted to understand how people can be so dedicated, and to see how through all their hardships, they persevered. With that kind of work, you don't always get good results. You have to be able to put up with disappointment and frustration, and to be patient. Susie had done this work for forty years, so that was very inspiring to me.

MOONEY: Thank you for sharing these stories. I will add that I've had similar experiences. What really made me appreciate the education I had was my first trip to Latin America, in 1994, when I was a junior at Yale studying psychology.

I grew up with a Spanish-speaking mother—she came to the United States fleeing communism in Cuba when she was twenty years old, and she married my father [an American] whom she met at The Catholic University of America. My mother always told me that there were educational opportunities in the U.S. that she didn't have in Cuba. But that never really sunk in until I myself went to Mexico and Cuba. I realized that in Mexico, many people didn't have public education, and others only had access to education up to the eighth grade. In Cuba that same summer of 1994, I realized that although the Cuban Revolution had expanded literacy and public schooling, it had come at the cost of freedom. As Amartya Sen, winner of the Nobel Prize in Economics, originally from India, has written, economic development should not come at the cost of human freedom. When I had the honor of meeting Amartya Sen in person, I asked him about Cuba's model of economic development. He remarked: What's the point of the Cuban government teaching everyone to read and then denying them the freedom to read any newspaper other than the government newspaper?

Then, as a graduate student in Sociology at Princeton, I traveled to Haiti in 2001 and 2002. I learned French and Haitian Creole. I visited schools in Haiti and sang songs with the children. There is tremendous material deprivation in Haiti. But many people in Haiti also have a kind of joy, and a deep sense of purpose, an ability to give and receive love easily.

The leaders of those communities are what you call moral exemplars. Part of what makes them leaders is that they know how to find that spark in every child and in every adult. The leaders may not have tons of money, but their commitment to their work and their ability to connect personally with people and inspire them to keep striving in spite of these difficult circumstances were attributes I wanted to emulate.

You have said that every child has a spark. Every child has a purpose. And you have written that character and moral education are the basis of any good education. Can you explain those concepts?

DAMON: There's both a general and an individual part to the spark every person has. The general spark is something that we all share as a species, which is that every child is born with a natural disposition toward empathy. Everyone has the potential to care for other people, and to share in their distress or joy. That's a very powerful moral predisposition. The role of learning is to develop this predisposition into its full potential.

In terms of the individual spark, every child has some special talent, or interest, or potential that is his or her own. It's the job of parents and teachers to help the child recognize what it is, and then allow the child the space and the freedom to explore. Once the child begins to express it, they must give the child resources—both material things and psychological encouragement—to develop that spark.

The need for a sense of purpose is something everyone shares, but in the particulars, everybody's purpose is unique. The only way children can develop their spark completely is by finding their own talents and interests, and discovering what it is they love to do, what they're capable of doing, and something they believe in—something they see as adding to the world. When a child discovers those three things, the child is ready to commit to a purposeful life.

The only way children can develop their spark completely is by finding their own talents and interests, and discovering what it is they love to do, what they're capable of doing, and something they believe in—something they see as adding to the world. When a child discovers those three things, the child is ready to commit to a purposeful life.

MOONEY: One of the key texts I teach in my courses on education is Jacques Maritain's book, *Education at the Crossroads.* Maritain reminds us that the real engine of education is the students themselves, because they have an inner spark. As a teacher, I've certainly experienced that, when you tap into a student's inner spark, the student really lights up.

To know where their talents are and discover where their aspirations lie, the students have to be exposed to learning a whole variety of subjects, right?

DAMON: Absolutely. I'm a big believer in liberal arts, meaning a general education. It's more important that even so-called computer nerds learn to appreciate great artwork, and that great artists learn to count and do math. In addition, everyone deserves a chance to go deep into something that they're especially good at. Educators need to provide people with the general knowledge that enables them to enjoy all of life and function well in society, and to allow people the freedom to go as far as they can in their own area of passion and talent.

Some have the perception that the liberal arts are only for the elite, because traditionally, liberal arts colleges have been elite institutions, but a broad education in the humanities is part of our right as citizens, all the way up through high school at least. Community colleges, too, play a very important role in making the liberal arts and humanities broadly available. These riches of life should not be limited to people of privilege.

MOONEY: Your work brings your knowledge of developmental psychology into the practice of education. Why is there relatively little research in the field of education on questions of morality and character? Why is moral education no longer central in how we think about what a good education is?

DAMON: Well, I think interest in morality and character in education are coming back. Let's recall that the early days of public education in our country were very focused on character and moral insights. The twentieth century moved away from that and education became increasingly specialized in an academic sense. People became a little threatened by the idea of teaching values to kids. Only in recent years has there been a recognition that we are teaching the whole child, including the child's character.

We're not just teaching logical thinking or academic knowledge or skills, but schools are responsible for educating the whole child. Even if you tried to avoid teaching values in school because they're controversial, if you're running a school, you actually do have to deal with values because you need to enforce or at least encourage honesty. You don't want kids cheating. You don't want children hurting each other. You want them to be orderly. You certainly don't want them to be discriminatory.

These are not controversial issues. Most American parents want their children to learn to be honest. This is a value that we can agree on, and the schools should promote.

MOONEY: What are some of are some of the important insights in moral and character education, and what are some of the big debates?

DAMON: Let me start with schooling itself—especially public schooling. One debate is very simply how much time should be devoted to non-academic or non-basic skills. This came up a lot in the last twenty years or so when school systems all over the country were encouraged, or even almost mandated by the federal government, to focus on basic skills at the exclusion of other kinds of knowledge or interests. Art, music, history, civics, and many other things started getting squeezed out of a lot of schools because there was such a demand to come up with good test scores in very narrow subject matters.

In that context, questions were raised about whether classroom discussions concerning character and moral issues were taking too much time away from learning how to do well on standardized tests. I think this was a misdirection for a lot of reasons, one of which being that morality and character formation were neglected in public education. Fortunately, we've learned that that was not a good approach, and in recent years, educators have been moving back to a whole-child perspective.

Another debate that comes up is *which* values should be taught in moral and character instruction. In returning to a whole-child perspective, there is a welcome new emphasis on social-emotional learning, moving into areas of development that go beyond basic skills. However, the question is whether or not values such as absolute right and wrong in moral issues should be emphasized.

It's a classic debate because you don't want teachers to be brainwashing children with specific beliefs about topics that are controversial in society. Still, there are some core values of common decency and civilized living that include honesty, compassion, fair-mindedness, responsibility, and respect. These are universal values that you find all over the world in every culture, and these are the values that should be included in the social-emotional realm. Teaching these values are very much a part of the educator's responsibility. Values that have to do with controversial areas that religion and cultures are divided on do not belong in the classroom. Schools need to focus on the common core values of civilizations everywhere.

MOONEY: In your 1988 book, *Moral Child,* you make the point that a lot of what children learn about morality is not learned in school. They learn it through real-life experiences with their parents, or in a civic group or a faith community, and so on.

So, would you say that it's not that some of these controversial issues around which religions and cultures differ shouldn't be considered part of an education more broadly, but the question is whether they belong in a public school classroom?

Damon: Yes, and of course, religious schools or any faith-based instruction ought to express their values and have the freedom to do so.

As you mentioned, experiential learning is how children develop much of their moral sense. Public schools, of course, have students from many cultures and religions, and in those contexts, it's important for teachers to focus on the values that are shared.

Mooney: How can some people uphold that there actually is an unchanging, universal tradition of values when a lot of people speak as if there is not? Is it possible ultimately to defend universal values without reference to religion?

Damon: Take the value of truth, for instance. Looking at human life in general, what would a relationship be like if you couldn't trust the other person to tell you the truth? Of course, that relationship would break down right away. You couldn't even communicate in any regular way. Values like truth-telling speak for themselves.

Whether you call it religion or another kind of faith, you should value people's lives, you should be compassionate, and you should be fair. These values seem to be self-evident for any kind of decent life. It is simply a commonsense approach.

Mooney: That's true, but people come to different conclusions on some ultimate questions of life. I think what you are saying is not that those differences in how people answer big questions don't exist or aren't consequential, but that in spite of those differences, there's a pretty large common basis of universal human morality that we can all draw on. In a country as diverse and as pluralistic as the United States, we should know what those similarities are (without ignoring the differences) and we should be thinking about teaching shared values. Is that a fair assessment of your thinking?

DAMON: Yes, and I think that this viewpoint about many common values has been validated by anthropologists and by people who study cultural psychology. As Richard Shweder, the cultural anthropologist and psychologist, puts it, there is moral universalism but not uniformity. In other words, there are cultural variations in values, as in other things, but there are some core beliefs that are necessary for civilizations, and that do span nearly all of them. Children learn these values by going to school, by being in families, by all kinds of instruction. It is our responsibility as adults to pass on these universal norms and wisdom to the young.

MOONEY: Many people want to go into education precisely to work with people very different from themselves in terms of race, religion, class or some other ascribed or chosen social marker. How does one teach universal values while also learning about the particularities of the context—racial, economic, geographical, religious and cultural—that one brings these ideas into?

DAMON: That's a difficult question to answer because I think it's important to pay attention to the particular character of each child. Every child has to find his or her own spark and own meaning in life, and these things most often don't follow group consciousness in any kind of way. We shouldn't stereotype people. An educator walking into a context different than one's own needs to get to know how to reach each child individually. That's the way to teach values—by connecting them to each child's spark and purpose, not to a group identity that hollows out individuality.

Mooney: In my teaching, I've worked with students from all kinds of backgrounds different than my own. In a pluralistic society, we should learn from our differences, I believe. That's why I would like us to have more opportunities to explore how the major world religions and philosophical traditions have answered life's fundamental questions. We shouldn't prevent ourselves from asking difficult questions just because not every tradition reaches the same answer. If we do that, we deprive students of their desire to talk about these questions from a variety of often competing perspectives. If I only talk to people who agree with me on big questions, then I may never see the gaps in my knowledge.

One of the major differences between you and other scholars in psychology or education comes out in your 2015 book, *The Power of Ideals*. You critique the reductionist view in much of social science for seeing the human person as purely material, or even just purely material and psychological. You assert that there's also a spiritual dimension to a person. Different faith traditions explain this spiritual aspect of being human in different ways, and you are trying to bring those questions back into education and psychology as part of who we are as humans.

You also say there are important insights on moral questions that we get from our own experience in the world, as well as from the ancient traditions of wisdom coming from philosophy and religion.

What you say may sound like common sense to many, but it seems you are reacting against a view that some hold that the only way to talk about right and wrong is through an experimental method that generates lots of data. You defend a pluralistic way of arriving at the truth, which includes collecting data from experiments, but also includes studying philosophical and religious traditions, and drawing inspiration from people who are moral exemplars.

DAMON: Yes. All research methods, taken by themselves, are inadequate. The best way to go about something is to try to combine and triangulate and get different views on the phenomena that you're studying.

There has been a recent trend in moral psychology to be reductionistic, which is to say that our moral responses are all based on our evolved biological processes. Some have gone so far as to apply a motivation of avoiding disgust to every kind of moral choice that people make. That's one kind of reductionism.

The other tendency, which is essentially the opposite, is to reduce everything we believe to whatever the so-called culture tells us. Our behavior is nothing but a response to what we've been told by whatever the rules of the game are that we've learned.

My view is that neither position explains the most important moral choices that people make. Our behavior is not just driven by a submerged biological impulse, and it's not just driven by our reading of cultural scripts. What explains people's choices are the mental processes, the agency they have—in a sense, the free will to make choices based on their beliefs and what inspires them. That's why Anne Colby and I called our book *The Power of Ideals*, because ideals really do make a difference in what we believe, and in our behavior.

To discover this principle of behavior motivated by ideals, we studied how moral exemplars make their choices. We looked at extraordinary people who have chosen to spend their lives pursuing noble purposes. That is a way of finding out what people are capable of doing—not only those we call moral exemplars, but also the potential we all have in our best moments. That's what we want to learn in studies of moral development.

That's exactly what psychology experiments do not do, the kind of experiments where you put people in a room and see how they'll respond if somebody shocks somebody. These experiments are very quick little snapshots of what ordinary people do when given an artificial situation. Such experiments don't go very deep into what people actually believe, and they don't study people who have really spent their lives thinking about values and making a moral commitment to certain values. Those moral exemplars are the people we're interested in—and they are people who learn and change, which an experimental snapshot also does not explore.

To be clear, not all of what an experiment concludes should be written off. If you take Philip Zimbardo's Stanford Prison Experiment as an example, we've learned that in certain conditions people are capable of cruel and authoritarian behavior. It's important to know that human nature has those tendencies, and that certain contexts bring them out in people. We've learned to be careful of those contexts, and to watch out for how people behave within them.

The things that we could not have learned from the experiment itself are that, first, people are capable of other things in these contexts, too. This includes refusing to behave in a cruel and authoritarian way, which many people have done, even under pressure. Also, many of the participants in the Zimbardo study engaged in a lot of reflection afterwards. Even Zimbardo himself learned that people are capable of acting better than his initial experiment showed.

What we don't always know from the conclusions of experiments are their limitations. And when the popular media covers dramatic results, they often simplify them, so sometimes the experimenters themselves present a fuller picture than you get on that little, thirty-second media coverage of them. We have to be careful of those simplifications.

Mooney: I often encourage people to not rely on soundbites, but to read some of the primary research and to listen to what a variety of scholars are saying about a topic. Experiments tell us something, but a person might behave one way today, then reflect on it and make a different choice tomorrow. The idea that the way people behave in an experimental condition with a snap judgment predicts how they're always going to behave strikes me as a really big conjecture. People reach their most deeply held moral commitments through struggle, reflection, and difficult experiences. Sometimes, people may even change what they believe and change how they behave.

No matter how many pieces of data you have, how many fMRIs or surveys or experiments, the results of those tools will not completely predict behavior. In addition, people talk about themselves as having freedom in their moral choices. They do not see their agency as being completely determined by a particular situation. Big data can't replace the biographical study of people, which shows how people sometimes revise or fundamentally change their views. Biographical studies allow us to see processes of struggle and to understand how people form moral commitments and live them out.

In your book on moral exemplars, you point out that even autobiographical self-reflection has its shortcomings. For example, we remember certain things more than others. There might be some missing pieces of our own stories we leave out. But that's not a sufficient reason to ignore a person's own reflections on his or her moral commitments. If we say what people do is completely irrelevant to what they believe, we've fallen into a kind of determinism about behavior.

Could you share an example of a moral exemplar from one of your studies to illustrate the process of how moral commitments are made?

DAMON: One of the early studies we did in the 1992 book *Some Do Care* profiled a woman named Virginia Durr, who grew up in Montgomery, Alabama. She began life with a lot of traditionally discriminatory attitudes, but she learned over time, especially at Wellesley College, to question her assumptions about how society should be structured, especially around race relations. She became a leader in the Civil Rights Movement through a lot of trial and error. She would try one thing and then learn that she needed to adjust her thinking in such and such a way. We interviewed her back in the 1980s when she was in her nineties.

One of the unique things about the human moral condition is that we learn. That's what the experiments don't give you a sense of. Human experiments are a snapshot, but human development is a movie. We have the capacity to learn from our mistakes—if we have the humility to be willing to question ourselves and to be open-minded.

The great Swiss psychologist Fritz Oser has done a number of studies on what he calls negative morality, which is showing how the most powerful thing in moral learning is when you confront the fact that you've done something wrong, and you have the humility to admit it. That's exactly where the study of biographies can help us understand how this kind of moral change happens.

MOONEY: In your courses, you have students interview a person. I do that in my courses, too. When students study someone's life in relationship to their social context, they see how complex human motivation is and how human behavior often changes over time.

One of the findings you discuss among moral exemplars is that growth and improvement often happen when we acknowledge failure, develop humility, and become more open-minded. You have written that part of character education and moral development has to be teaching students to understand where they've fallen and helping them to grow from their failures. Why is incorporating that into education so important? And why is it such a difficult thing to do today?

DAMON: At the heart of the problem is a misdirected message: the idea that self-esteem, in and of itself, is a value that should be automatically passed along to students. Of course, students should be encouraged, feel valued, and have confidence in their potential, so it's important that teachers and parents communicate a sense of optimism and self-regard. But that doesn't mean to give students the message that anything they do is automatically right, or that they should not be corrected when they make mistakes.

Ironically, when students think that you're giving them phony praise, like "everybody's a winner" or "there's no such thing as making a mistake," then they discount it. That does not build their self-esteem. What does build self-esteem is the sense that, "Well, I may not have done it this time. I may have made a mistake or failed at this particular thing, but I can get back up on the horse and ride it again." That's the message that students need to learn.

> Self-esteem truly is a ***particular*** message that encourages students to achieve, and to try to do better. It gives them the confidence that they can persevere and succeed. Educators need to communicate that excellence in something requires having the discipline to actually practice and to do the hard work of mastering that skill.

That has been a problem in education, because people are confused about what self-esteem is and how children really learn it. Self-esteem truly is a *particular* message that encourages students to achieve, and to try to do better. It gives them the confidence that they can persevere and succeed. Educators need to communicate that excellence in something requires having the discipline to actually practice and to do the hard work of mastering that skill.

Furthermore, discipline is needed in a behavioral sense, too. If you cheat in school, for example, you should have to do the work over again, or a privilege should be removed, in order to pass along the message that your behavior was wrong and you need to learn to do better. We're not automatically programmed to do the right thing without some effort, so it's very important to get honest feedback from people who have the responsibility to tell you when you are doing something that needs to be corrected.

MOONEY: Every child has a spark, every child has a talent, but they're not going to be able to reach that potential or develop that talent without structure, discipline, feedback, and guidance. Part of education has to be educating the student to know how to hear that message and persevere.

In these instances of moral exemplars who've done extraordinary things, how much of that is attributable to their individual spark and how much to the general spark that everyone has?

DAMON: The personal sparks derive from the actual forms of action that they do, and the causes that they're choosing to commit to. They understand something about a problem that needs to be fixed because they themselves have lived it, recognized it, or been interested in it.

The general characteristics that they all share, which we can all learn from, are things like courage and commitment, and the special combination of humility and certainty. It truly is a very inspiring and unusual combination. They're humble enough to learn, and they often say, "Well, people call me a leader, but I'm actually following by learning from people that think of themselves as my followers." These people are so open-minded!

They're open-minded in the sense of always learning, but they never question the goals of compassion or justice that they're committed to. They're so certain about these values that you cannot deter them even by threats. They have this wonderful combination of humility that regulates their behavior and certainty that keeps them on track.

MOONEY: So, although the particular circumstances of their lives or their particular talents might be unique, we can learn from how they lived out virtues like courage, humility, and open-mindedness. Through studying their lives, we can think about how to apply those virtues in our own lives. I would add that actually choosing to be around moral exemplars is a way of learning from other people's life experiences and the values or virtues that we want to emulate.

Are there models for a kind of education built on reading and studying moral exemplars?

DAMON: Yes, morals were the heart of the liberal arts tradition as envisioned by John Henry Newman in the nineteenth century. He wrote systematically about what became the liberal tradition in education, centered on the moral dilemmas that people face. However, academia drifted away from that in the twentieth century, as it became more specialized and more hidebound in terms of disciplines.

Students have lost interest in some of the humanities because they aren't being taught in a true liberal arts fashion. We should recapture the central human dramas and moral components that the humanities like English literature and the great works of fine art deal with, and we should discuss them in the classroom.

There are ways that some schools are already doing this. Some colleges have put on campus-wide trials of Socrates, with students playing different roles to enact these moral debates. This is the kind of creative re-animation that we should be doing more.

Mooney: It is important to talk about moral exemplars because what we need in difficult times is hope. Hope often comes from looking at people who have led courageous lives, and learning from them.

I see a movement to return to education based on character development, morality, and discussing deep philosophical questions. I have met moral exemplars who are teachers in very difficult urban contexts or low-income contexts in the U.S. and abroad. I am moved by those teachers and administrators, whether they are in public schools, private schools, or are homeschooling. They are passionate about educating students of all backgrounds in a liberal arts tradition and the work they are doing has a tremendous impact on society because so much of our life in common depends on how we educate the young.

But some critics of the liberal arts tradition might say that only someone who doesn't have to worry about getting a job, to put it bluntly, has the time to sit around and think about purpose and morality. What would you say to someone who sees a liberal arts education as a luxury for the privileged?

Damon: In all of our studies of purpose at all ages, from adolescence to the early adult years up through the senior population, we have found that regardless of socioeconomic, ethnic, or other demographic factors, people see their lives as having purpose. The desire for purpose is present equally across all the different marker categories we commonly use to demarcate privilege of one kind or another.

It's easy to see why purpose is a universal human need: purpose provides the same benefits for everybody, and it doesn't matter where you are on the socioeconomic ladder. A purposeful life brings with it the benefits of resilience, energy, motivation, and meaning. People everywhere recognize that, and so they search for purpose. To the extent they find it, it's not determined by anything having to do with background. Seeking and obtaining purpose is a universal human capacity that is available to people everywhere.

Purpose can be very ordinary, too. It doesn't have to be something fancy or noble. You have a purpose when you want to raise your children; that's an ordinary purpose that people everywhere have. Purpose does not have to be something intellectual, or high-status. Every vocation has a purpose.

MOONEY: A liberal arts education is centered on educating the young to both master certain kinds of knowledge and to find their purpose. That's what makes it a universal approach to education.

DISCUSSION QUESTIONS

1. Damon talks about the importance of learning at home and learning at school. In what ways do those two learning environments complement each other? Can they come into conflict? If so, how?

2. Identify a moral exemplar who has influenced your life. Why do you admire him/her? What are his/her virtues?

3. Do you agree with Damon that developing one's potential and finding one's spark is readily accessible to everyone, regardless of class, race, privilege, etc.?

4. What sort of difficult questions do you find the education system to be poor at addressing, or in neglects to address altogether? What are the ramifications?

5. What struggles have you gone through, or have seen others go through, that have been formative for shaping your core beliefs?

6. Name an instance when you engaged in negative morality by virtue of a mistake you made. How might you (or have you) learned from that mistake?

7. What do you think it might mean to fail gracefully at something? What are the merits of failure, especially if you respond to it appropriately?

8. How are the moral life and the intellectual life related? For example, is moral humility—admitting one's failures—related to intellectual humility—the ability to learn from others and be willing to change our minds when given good reasons?

9. Mooney states, "Every child has a spark, every child has a talent, but they're not going to be able to reach that potential or develop that talent without structure, discipline, feedback, and guidance. Part of education has to be educating the student to know how to hear that message and persevere." What are some ways in which you have seen education provide discipline, feedback, and guidance? What are some examples where it has failed to do that? What does it take for the student to "know how to hear" that realizing his/her spark requires discipline and feedback?

10. How should teachers teach universal values in a public school compared to a private and/or religious school setting? Does acknowledging that different traditions answer moral questions differently always imply moral relativism—that there are no true answers to moral questions?

REFERENCES

Colby, Anne, and William Damon. *Some Do Care.* New York: Free Press, 1994.

Damon, William. *The Moral Child: Nurturing Children's Natural Moral Growth.* New York: Free Press, 1990.

_____. *The Path to Purpose: How Young People Find Their Calling in Life.* New York: Free Press, 2009.

_____., and Anne Colby. *The Power of Ideals: The Real Story of Moral Choice.* Oxford: Oxford University Press, 2015.

"Fritz Oser." International Academy of Education, 2015, at www.iaoed.org/index.php/fellows/item/53-fritz-oser

Maritain, Jacques. *Education at the Crossroads.* New Haven: Yale University Press, 1960.

Newman, John Henry. *The Idea of a University Defined and Illustrated: In Nine Discourses Delivered to the Catholics of Dublin.* Chicago: Loyola University Press, 1927.

Sen, Amartya. *Development as Freedom.* New York: Anchor, 2000.

Shweder, Richard. "Relativism and Universalism." In *A Companion to Moral Anthropology*, edited by Didier Fassin. Hoboken: Wiley-Blackwell, 2012.

Shweder, Richard A. *Thinking Through Cultures: Expeditions in Cultural Psychology*. Cambridge: Harvard University Press, 1991.

Zimbardo, Philip G. "Stanford Prison Experiment." Stanford Prison Experiment, 1999, at www.prisonexp.org.

ADDITIONAL READINGS

Damon. William "Why We Can't All Just Get Along." Hoover Institution, June 4, 2012, at www.hoover.org/research/why-we-cant-all-just-get-along.

_____. "Bringing in a New Era in Character Education." Hoover Institution, January 1, 2002, at www.hoover.org/research/bringing-new-era-character-education.

_____. *Failing Liberty 101: How We Are Leaving Young Americans Unprepared for Citizenship in a Free Society*. Stanford: Hoover Institution Press, 2011.

_____. *Greater Expectations: Overcoming the Culture of Indulgence in Our Homes and Schools*. New York: Free Press, 1996.

_____. "Restoring Purpose and Patriotism to American Education." Fordham Institute, March 11, 2020, at www.fordhaminstitute.org/national/commentary/restoring-purpose-and-patriotism-american-education.

_____. "The Death of Honesty." Hoover Institution, May 5, 2014, at www.hoover.org/research/death-honesty-0.

_____. "The Education of Steve Jobs." Hoover Institution, September 16, 2011, at www.hoover.org/research/education-steve-jobs.

_____. "A Curriculum for the Curious." Hoover Institution, January 23, 2012, at www.hoover.org/research/curriculum-curious.

Mooney, Margarita. "Newman's Vision of Liberal Arts Education." Margarita Mooney, May 7, 2018, at http://margaritamooney.com/2018/05/newmans-vision-of-liberal-arts-education/.

≈

Elizabeth Corey is an associate professor of Political Science at Baylor University, in Waco, Texas. Her writing has appeared in a variety of popular and scholarly journals, including *First Things*, *National Affairs*, and *The Wall Street Journal*. She received a bachelor's degree in Classics from Oberlin College, and a master's degree in Art History and master's and doctoral degrees in Political Science from Louisiana State University. She was the American Enterprise Institute's Values and Capitalism Visiting Professor in 2018–2019. She serves on the Board of Directors of the Institute on Religion and Public Life, publisher of *First Things*.

CHAPTER 3

Learning in Love: Authentic Friendships and Liberal Learning

ELIZABETH COREY *and* MARGARITA A. MOONEY

MOONEY: Could you tell us about your educational background?

COREY: I began as a very devoted piano major at Oberlin Conservatory. I was certain as a young person that the only worthwhile thing to do with one's life was to become a professional musician. I was about two years in at the conservatory and realized that this was probably not the career or life for me—not because I didn't love it, but because it had become so professionalized.

Luckily, Oberlin has a great liberal arts program, and I switched my major from music to classics. I thought, "Well, if I'm not going to do music, I might as well start at the beginning." I ended up doing a full classics degree, but in my last semester I took an art history class. I then discovered that I had been missing out all these years on my true love, which was art history. I went on to do a master's in medieval art history on early Christian art at Louisiana State University. In my last semester I took a political science seminar on a whim. Right after, I did a master's and a Ph.D. in political science, which was not at all what I had planned.

It was, to use Michael Oakeshott's famous phrase, the pursuit of intimations: finding things that you are interested in and following where those lead. At the end of it all, I landed in political science. I worked on American politics, but more so on political theory. Now, I am at Baylor with my husband, who is also a professor here.

Mooney: The first article of yours that I read has the same name as this series, "Learning in Love." When people think about liberal learning, they are not usually thinking about love. Why did you write it? What do you hope that people take away from it?

Corey: I wrote the piece back in 2014, in reaction to a report called "The Heart of the Matter," a manifesto about the importance of learning the humanities. I found it full of platitudes and empty words, talking about the importance of liberal education in a way that made me think, "If this were supposed to encourage people to go toward the liberal arts it would do the exact opposite. I would rather not be involved in this at all."

I asked myself what *did* interest me in the liberal arts, and realized that there were a number of people who modeled for me a life that was attractive to me. I wondered, "If I'm not going be a musician, then maybe there's something here in this world of learning that I've missed, and that is worth pursuing."

This is how people grow to love liberal arts, not by being told that it's good for you or that everybody should have a certain education because that's what civilized people do. It is to be "evangelized," to be shown, to be led, to be brought to an understanding of why reading these books and thinking and talking in these ways is important in itself.

That is best modeled through person-to-person conversation: in the classroom, in the seminar room, in the living room. So many professors do this, like inviting students to their homes to have tea or a meal.

Suddenly, the life of learning isn't just this thing you do at college only, but in every aspect of your life.

MOONEY: You ask people to ask themselves, "Who taught you to fall in love with the subject?"—not "What did you learn in school?" The best educators are people who love their subject and come into the classroom to communicate that love. That inspiration is truly something that students don't forget.

COREY: For me, it was a family friend, a professor at Louisiana State University who was not *my* professor, but would sit and talk with me for hours about vocation and the relative merits of different kinds of lives. Together we would read Plato and Michael Oakeshott, about whom I ended up writing a dissertation. We would do all of this reading and talking, and more reading and talking. It was magical.

That's something I try now to reproduce with my own students, but it takes a kind of humility and charity. Really, what's the reward for a teacher who does this kind of intensive work? There isn't any. The university doesn't really recognize it. Nonetheless, the people who have been most influential in my life are the people who do this kind of thing. It arises not from some kind of professionalism, but out of love for students and love for other people.

MOONEY: Sadly, a lot of people have fallen out of love with learning, since learning has become a tool for achievement. Maybe a second question we need to ask students to honestly ask themselves is, "Why did you fall out of love with learning?" That leads me to your piece "Achievement and the Christian Life," written for the American Enterprise Institute Initiative on Faith and Public Life.

What is the risk when learning becomes nothing but a way to brag about what your grades were or what kind of fellowship you got? What happens when the end of learning becomes achievement and love disappears? What do we need to do to rethink this achievement culture that we've created?

COREY: I teach in the Honors College, and as you can guess, the Honors College brings in the most highly talented students at Baylor. They get a semester or so in, and they start feeling really stressed. Sometimes they come to me and say, "I don't know if I can do all this. I'm exhausted. I know that I need to do the internship during the summer, and I need to be involved in this society and this other group of events on campus. But I question what it's all for."

As they get older, the pressure gets even more intense. What will they be doing after college? They're constantly being encouraged to facilitate their career prospects by doing X and Y, and there is no time for leisure, no real time for contemplation during this rat race that is set up in the very beginning of college. The piece arose out of many conversations with high-achieving young people who started to say, "What am I doing all this work for? What is the end goal of all this?" I wanted to offer some alternatives.

David Brooks has written about this, with his distinction between the résumé and the eulogy virtues. That's a very nice way of putting it. What are people going to say about you at your funeral? Do you want them to say that you wrote seventeen books or that you were a wonderful person and a devoted mother, or any number of other personal goals you might pursue? Of course, I try to make the case that there is a place for both of these things, but we need to reorient the way we think about achievement so that it doesn't become the only goal of life.

MOONEY: You mentioned that times of crisis in our personal lives can make us rethink achievement. For me that moment was probably my father's unexpected passing during graduate school, which happened right around 9/11. I asked myself, "Why am I even bothering to do a Ph.D.? Why does the life of the mind matter when there's this huge world crisis going on right now?" I really struggled with that.

What I did is I started organizing small reading groups with my fellow graduate students from my department, or from one of the Christian ministries on campus. This is part of how Scala eventually came to be. One of the books that helped me rethink my own approach to life and to learning was Josef Pieper's *Leisure: The Basis of Culture* (1948).

COREY: This book is one of the best. Pieper argues that we've forgotten how to be leisurely. He sets out various definitions that are not the "real" understanding of leisure. It's not, "I'm going to spend my leisure time sitting on my back porch with a drink in my hand." Leisure is not mere rest, or rest so that you can do more work in the future. It is a categorically different kind of activity from work, and it requires a contemplative attitude that has to be cultivated. You have to learn what it is, why it's attractive, and then how to do it.

He contrasts that with where we are now, what he calls a world of "total work"; all of our striving is oriented toward work, achievement, money-making, honor. We want to be published in the best places. We want to be at the best schools. We want to be at the best companies. We want to be constantly more and more excellent. Pieper finds this striving to be a rather dreadful way of living. He makes a distinction between the person as a "functionary" and the person as a "full human being" who can observe the Sabbath and celebrate and understand what leisure is. He also talks about how hard it is to cultivate that attitude in the present day.

My other very important influence in thinking about achievement is Michael Oakeshott, a British political philosopher who lived from 1901 to 1990. Throughout his work, he meant to show the limits of achievement in human life. His 1993 book *Religion, Politics, and the Moral Life* includes essays that were found after his death in his desk drawer. One of these little essays is called "Work and Play." Here he makes a very deep, Pieperian distinction between work as something we do to satisfy wants: it is first to satisfy needs but then to satisfy wants. Work never ends because we're constantly looking for the next thing, and after we get that next thing, then we're looking for the next, next thing.

Oakeshott contrasts play with the endless satisfaction of wants. Play consists in love, friendship, conversation, liberal learning, artistic aesthetic experience—all these things that the liberal arts try to promote.

I was very captured by that. In the world of classical music, where I came from, it's all about achievement. Hopefully you still love the playing of music, but a lot of times you do not because you're just trying to get to the next level. Reading Pieper and Oakeshott, I realized, "Well, there are other things to do with one's life than just to achieve and to achieve and to achieve."

MOONEY: That's why I've been doing these reading groups for all these years. I realized that I am an overachiever and I need help; I need a support group to read these ideas and study them.

A lot of literature that questions the achievement culture focuses on work-life balance. How much time are you giving to different aspects of your life? But what Pieper and Oakeshott are saying is that balance is not just about how many hours go to work. Rather, what's the state of mind that you're bringing both into your work and into your rest? We get habituated to a certain way of being in the world. Often even when I would block off the time to do non-work things, it was incredibly difficult to slow down my mind because I was in overdrive. Pieper and Oakeshott are challenging us not just to change our time allocation, but to change ourselves from the inside out.

I've done that through practicing my faith, and also through more intentionally cultivating time alone in nature or with friends at art museums. I came to see this view of leisure as part of my education because it's part of forming me as a person.

Do you find that you get to apply these ideas to your work as a professor? For your students, is it actually possible to live in this leisurely way?

Corey: It is very hard to do in the modern world, and it's harder the older you get and the more responsibilities you have. The world pushes us toward constant activity, attention to emails and text messages and all the demands of all the people we know in our lives.

I always ask my students if there anything is that they do for its own sake, such as a class that they've loved that wasn't going to affect their future prospect for a career. That's getting to the kind of leisure that Pieper and Oakeshott are talking about, doing something without a thought for what's going to follow it. Listening to music is usually that. We do have experiences of these leisured modes of activity, it's just that almost all of us get in this compulsive, list-making mode, and it's very hard to get out of it.

I'm not only trying to show younger people the futility of a life based on achievement, but to show that there are ways of thinking about achievement that are, frankly, better for your soul. One of them is to see your desire to achieve as being inspired by a vision of the good. If, let's say, you want to be a professional musician, why do you want to do that? You could say, "Because I want to be famous," or you can say, "Because I want to achieve excellence and beauty."

One other way of thinking about achievement is also to say, "Well, it's not just about what I do through hard work and perseverance; it's also about discernment of my own gifts." Whatever I do with my life, it's not wholly mine. It's given to me by God.

Ultimately, in the highest things, you end up not thinking about yourself. Once you become excellent at something, whether that's teaching or writing or being a tax attorney or being a doctor, you're actually looking for the good of other people. It's about how you make the lives of others better and encourage them in their pursuits.

I'm not only trying to show younger people the futility of a life based on achievement, but to show that there are ways of thinking about achievement that are, frankly, better for your soul. One of them is to see your desire to achieve as being inspired by a vision of the good.

MOONEY: So it's not that achievement or utility in and of themselves are bad, but that if they're the highest end, then we've gone too far. C. S. Lewis's 1939 essay "Learning in War-Time" makes the point that, from a faith perspective, the good that we do through our academic life is secondary. The primary thing is trying to conform our minds to the good that God wills.

I always tell people that if you want to do a Ph.D., get prepared to feel totally useless! It's extremely humbling to write an original piece of scholarship because most of what you write ends up in the trash bin. However, sometimes, somehow something eventually comes through. That's when you realize that the best we can do with our minds is not only to try to achieve, but also be open to mystery and grace.

You taught a course for the American Enterprise Institute called "Defending Disinterest" and wrote a wonderful piece on defending disinterest in the university. It's similar to a piece you published in the *Chronicle of Higher Education* with a wonderfully provocative title: "The University Has No Purpose." What are these two modes of the university you describe?

Corey: "Defending Disinterest" comes out of a notion called modality, which was a big idea of Michael Oakeshott's. Imagine a water bottle. If I were to hold one in my hand and ask what it is, what's the first answer you would give?

It would probably be something like, "This is a conveyance to get water to my mouth. I want a drink and this holds water, and so I'm going to use it for that reason." This is the practical mode, which has to do with desires and aversions and things that attract us and things we want to avoid.

But I could ask the question again, and you could answer in a different mode that a water bottle is a thing made of polymers. It has molecules and atoms. You could say there's a scientific way of looking at this, which is categorically different from the first answer. Or you could give a historical answer, maybe say this is the modern version of the Thracian drinking horn.

Finally, you could say, "It's an object of beauty with curvy lines that are attractive to the eye and it has a captivating translucence." These four examples show a kind of modal understanding. The dominant one is the practical mode, but you've got aesthetic, historical, scientific, and maybe many more.

Likewise, there are ways of looking at university education in different modes. We are all quite familiar with two iterations of the practical mode. One is the university as a means to a flourishing economic life.

The other is as a vehicle for advocating certain political and social causes. Jonathan Haidt has called this a social-justice university. For both of these, your time at the university is understood as a means to something else that you will go on and do later.

Against all that, I argue that we ought to understand the university as "disinterested." Let's use our time to understand what is out there to be understood. Let's read great books. Let's learn math. Let's explore science. Let's do all the things that a university affords for us without thinking about how to use this in the future. Let's enjoy.

Can these two different understandings of a university coexist? Some people say no, you've got to do either one or the other, but I'm hoping that at many universities there is a place for both.

The problem is that often universities don't understand the disinterested kind of learning. They want everything to be relevant to the present day and to the economic concerns of the surrounding area or to the pursuit of science. They're always looking for ways to relate what's going on at the university to these practical goals.

MOONEY: How might this notion of the university as a place of disinterest look for students for whom achievement might be more important given their socio-economic background of limited resources?

COREY: Here's where I do think those two ends can coexist. I'm not saying that the students shouldn't do anything useful after college, or that they shouldn't try to have really great careers. I hope they do. What I am arguing is that achievement can coexist with an intensive liberal arts, conversational, disinterested education.

The danger often lies with the students' parents. My husband and I often do orientation talks for Baylor, and parents will say, "I'm worried that any time that's spent in this 'uselessness' is going to harm my son or daughter. Why would he take the time out to read these books that seem to have nothing to do with his or her future life?"

What we say in response is that it's not all about career; the questions that come up in these books are, "What is love? What is a worthwhile life? How should I approach death? Is there life after death?" To say that those questions are not important does not do justice to the full humanity of our students.

MOONEY: What are the pitfalls of the activist model of education?

COREY: I'm skeptical about activism both from the left and from the right. Either one is essentially making the end of university education something other than the education itself. For instance, at Oberlin, people say, "Activism looks like this: we are going to embrace the left-leaning political causes. Our classes are going to revolve around that, and we are going to equip you to go out and make a difference in the world in ways that we've preordained to be correct."

What really ought to be going on at a university is that students hear a lot of different perspectives, even on controversial current issues. The aim is not to go out and change the world immediately, but first to better understand the conditions that are making our world as it is.

MOONEY: You say in your article on the disinterested university that we need less of "rage readings." What do you mean by this?

COREY: How often do we read things that we disagree with simply to say how wrong they are? I started to see how Twitter works, and it turns out a lot of what goes on there is people being angry at other people for saying things they don't like. That kind of thing is really a waste of intellectual energy. Not that you shouldn't disagree vehemently with others, but I don't want people to read something simply to hate it.

MOONEY: I sometimes struggle with this when I'm teaching authors who I know I ultimately don't agree with. When we're teaching a book or discussing an important issue in the mode of education, we're actually trying to learn what somebody is saying before we enter into critique or rage.

What I've seen, and what so many faculty and students tell me, is that on college campuses students often pick the most outrageous quote possible to discredit somebody we disagree with, or students, and sometimes faculty, affirm a particular term or word or position without any analysis.

I'm a person of faith who identifies as more conservative, and I care deeply about social justice. My work has been on immigration from Haiti and Mexico and on people with mental illness and drug addiction in the U.S. There are really complex question around all of those issues, yet I have found at times that it is difficult environment to have an open debate about different ways of responding to pressing social problems.

How do you create an environment where these dialogues can happen?

COREY: The answer will change according to the subject matter. For example, I teach a seminar class called Great Texts and Art. We read E. H. Gombrich's wonderful 1950 book *The Story of Art* as we look at art across the ages. We do a lot of talking in the course about why an artist might convey something in such a way.

I also teach Introduction to Constitutional Law, which surveys the major landmark cases in American legal history. We read the cases with the dissents and the concurrences. Here it's different from my art history class because we talk about more contentious issues. We look at affirmative action, racism, abortion, presidential power, and any number of other things. To do this successfully, I lay down ground rules, saying, "Look, we're going to be talking about things that you might already have an opinion about. How can we do this in such a way that we are not going to take offense at the view that is raised by somebody who you disagree with?" Once the rules are in place, the conversation tends to go really well.

This whole notion of disinterest allows you to freely ask these questions. It doesn't mean you hold those views. I always tell my students, "Look, in a seminar I don't necessarily think what you say is what you always believe, but in engaging an author seriously and in trying to understand what that author is saying, you can postulate things, and you can ask questions, and you can say things that you might not say out of the classroom." What matters is trying to get at what these authors are trying to convey and the way they're trying to convey it.

That's something only a university can provide because everywhere else, there are consequences.

Mooney: A lot of discussion also revolves around students' identities, and often around a particular race, class, or sexual identification. How do you maintain what's good about integrating one's identity with learning while not falling into identity politics, where our identity is detached from reason?

Corey: I find that great texts are the best way of dealing with that. I'll use an example from the *Aeneid*. In the love affair of Dido and Aeneas, Dido kills herself because Aeneas leaves her. Sometimes the young men in the class will say, "I was much more like Dido in my last relationship," or the women will say, "I was kind of like Aeneas." What I like about these remarks is that these students identify not so much with their race or their sex or their class, but rather with the human experiences in the book.

MOONEY: In a Scala reading group we tackled Plato's *Symposium* and discussed its different ways of understanding love. I'm not trained formally in the classics, but it was exciting to grapple with that book because I thought, "This is totally out of my wheelhouse. Yet, it allows me to explore my identity and my understanding of love in a context different than mine."

In some ways, shifting the context depoliticizes the question of identity because we're not trying to discover our identity with reference to one or another currently salient political question.

One of the concerns I have with the activist model of education is that if the end of education is to change our current world, then there's almost no reason to study the past other than perhaps to critique it. There's no concept that history or tradition has some intrinsic value in being understood.

I think we need teachers who can show how the classics like Plato and Augustine help us get to fundamental human questions that are timeless. To have a coherent identity, the human person needs to connect their own interior life and social location to the past, present, and future.

Is this model of disinterested education, where our special gifts become the way we serve others, possible in our current system where self-interest is touted so highly?

COREY: I think it is possible. However, because we are constantly concerned about our lives and our future prospects—all of these very normal and appropriate concerns—it seems almost artificial to do what I'm asking in disinterested education, but it's very valuable. It requires us to set aside those very pressing human interests for a while.

Could we read Plato without thinking, "How will this affect contemporary politics?" Could we understand him in his own words and in his own time, and take some joy in doing that? Granted, there will be personal implications. I'm constantly reflecting on the books I read with respect to myself, and I think many students do too. I have to tell myself, "If I read Plato, then maybe I can understand Plato."

This is the model of education at St. John's College: an interval of time when the practical questions are set aside. The problem with that model in the contemporary university is that so few people now have any experience of it, so they find it weird. You have to make a very strong argument for "the usefulness of useless knowledge," as Abraham Flexner puts it.

MOONEY: In the essay "A Place of Learning," Oakeshott argues that the human being interprets himself or herself in various modes. You mentioned some of these: economic, political, theological, and biological.

Although a liberal arts mode of education is often contrasted with a social justice model of education, could it be that a liberal arts model or a disinterested approach to learning is precisely the mode of education that does the most justice because it is most in accord with our human nature?

COREY: I've never thought about it in those terms! Oakeshott identifies all sorts of modes in which we can understand human experience, and it is the job of a university to expose students to that. But what are we doing in so many cases now? We are exposing them only to the most practical, utilitarian ways of viewing the world.

I think it does most justice to the fullness of the human condition to take all these diverse modes into account, rather than just making education sterile job training or political activism.

MOONEY: How do you understand the place of diversity in education?

COREY: The problem with the use of diversity right now is that it ascribes too much of a person's identity to the characteristics that are only part of our identity as humans. People assume a lot about me because I'm a woman in academia. They think I must be pretty liberal, and they're surprised when I say, "Actually, I'm pretty conservative." That's an assumption people make about me based on my membership in a group. To generalize on this basis is really doing a disservice to my or any person's own ability to think independently or to express views other than those expected. We need intellectual diversity to keep us honest; we need a wider diversity of political and religious viewpoints on campus.

The genius of a university is its wide range of people all teaching their own subjects, talking with each other, appealing to the different loves of the students while having different loves of their own, and modeling that for the students.

MOONEY: In the classroom, I have found that what students are really eager for is to get beyond the typical way we think about diversity as putting people into one or another large social group and to actually get to know people for who they are personally. This is all without denying that in certain instances, the color of your skin or being a woman does tell you something really important. Nicanor Austriaco has argued that a classical liberal arts education should help students bring their many sources of identity into their learning but integrate them using their reason.

How do you cultivate friendships centered on the life of the mind in the classroom that acknowledge students' many sources of identity in a way that builds unity, not fragmentation?

Corey: Relating to people's very diverse experiences requires a willingness to try to throw yourself into the mind and heart of somebody who is not you. Sometimes it is the hardest thing in the world to say, "I need to see the world through this person's eyes, somebody who I don't agree with or don't even like." Still, to try to understand the world as he or she sees it is the best thing for cultivating friendships.

By doing so, you can begin to explore why you might even have a reason to like him or her. A fundamental attitude of both humility about your own views and charity toward others is the best foundation for friendship.

My best friends from Oberlin are very far from me as I am a pretty conservative woman. They hold views on things that I don't agree with; I hold views that they don't agree with. However, the beauty of the world prior to social media and technology as it is now is that we could make friendships with a broader array of people than we do now.

Today we are constantly encouraged and encouraging others to post this inflammatory article or tweet something provocative. It closes off the possibility of friendships with people who are quite different from you.

Mooney: College orientation programs focus on things like picking your classes, but there are also often orientation programs aimed at risky behaviors like excessive drinking and sexual harassment. What if college orientation programs raised questions like: what does authentic friendship look like, what is a good marriage, what is love?

COREY: Students are dying for adults—and not simply their parents—to talk to them about important things that have to do with love, like potential marriage, and what life is like after college. What does a flourishing adult life look like? At the Baylor Honors College, we've even had some seminars on love, marriage, and dating!

MOONEY: Is it hard to have personal relationships with students when certain groups are demonized on campuses because they fall out of line with a supposedly orthodox view on something? How is it possible to build authentic friendships when on many campuses people are hostile and suspicious of one another?

COREY: It has become infinitely harder to navigate these matters in the last ten years or so. While Title IX has done some good things, it's also made it such that personal relationships are looked at as potential sources of danger. The loss in not being able to have those kinds of close relationships, especially between professors and students, is substantial.

In this day and age, we can be intentional about having students over with our families, going to church with them, or meeting at the Starbucks on campus. Getting out of the classroom or the teacher's office—any of these official spaces that make us see each other only as teacher and student—is very beneficial. There are ways of making it work.

MOONEY: The kind of friendships and intimacy you're talking about don't only have to happen one-on-one. Sometimes, it's easier for me as a practical matter to get a group of students together and share a lunch. I have found that in small groups, the conversation really can be personal. While in a classroom setting students might start to become more political and feel defensive, in smaller groups that's actually rarely the case.

This brings us back to the importance of leisure, about slowing down the mind and reflecting on your interior to be able to enter into those conversations. We should not always enter an encounter with the motive of debating or putting down another's views, which is really wearing on students' friendships at college right now. We should learn to listen, to really understand, first.

A deeper point that Pieper makes is that the achievement culture we live in is self-centered. Love, by contrast, is self-transcendent. That is key to developing authentic friendships—friendships that aren't about utility, but rather about deep connection, about seeing the other person as he or she is and wants to be seen.

Do students feel that their friendships have become weakened to this achievement culture?

A deeper point that Pieper makes is that the achievement culture we live in is self-centered. Love, by contrast, is self-transcendent. That is key to developing authentic friendships—friendships that aren't about utility, but rather about deep connection, about seeing the other person as he or she is and wants to be seen.

COREY: Certainly, in some parts of the university, friendships are about networking. That is a very utilitarian understanding of friendship. We subtly encourage students to view everyone as a potential help or hindrance in your long-term plans.

Ideally, the end of friendship is not using the friend for any purpose, but delighting in the friend.

MOONEY: C. S. Lewis is another great go-to to learn about authentic friendship, especially his 1960 book *The Four Loves.*

What are some habits to cultivate that help break through the self-interested, achievement-oriented culture that keep what's good about achievement while also promoting habits and routines that foster leisure and love?

COREY: Get up early, carve out a few minutes or hopefully an hour of time for yourself. You can read devotional literature, you can read Pieper, you can read really anything you want to. I find that if I don't do something early before everyone else is up, I lose my leisure. Something else I do with my husband, who's also an academic, is a cocktail hour every evening!

Also, of course, you can keep the Sabbath (which I'm often not very good at doing). Set aside a day that is simply not about your work and not about you and is a day of celebration. Pieper talks about celebration as a very vital part of life; it is essential to the soul.

MOONEY: Over time, I have established one, two, or maybe three daily routines to keep my inner life strong, from meditating on the Psalms to daily Mass or reading a devotional book. When I keep those practices, my day goes better. How does your Christian faith relate to your love for the liberal arts? Is there some intrinsic link between faith, love, beauty, and art?

COREY: I do think this notion of achievement and the worry about making a mark in the world looks different from the perspective of the Christian faith. In other words, if you are not a believer, if you're not looking for a kind of transcendence that comes through Christ, it's hard to understand how achievement is as unimportant as I'm saying it is.

Achievement is good insofar as it's a part of human life, but I understand there to be greater purposes in life than personal achievement. Christianity says the same thing. It's not about you, and it's not about what you do on your own. Rather, it's your submission to a God who cares about you and who hopes for your eternal salvation.

DISCUSSION QUESTIONS

1. Corey states that developing a love for learning often comes through a person who takes a vested interest in you and gives of himself/herself to help you grow in this way. She describes this as being "evangelized." Can you think of anybody or any times when you were "evangelized" in this way? Who was your favorite/most influential teacher and why?

2. Corey states, "What really ought to be going on at a university is that students hear a lot of different perspectives, even on controversial current issues. The aim is not to go out and change the world immediately, but first to better understand the conditions that are making our world as it is." In what ways have many universities "jumped the gun" in pursuing societal change, rather than staying within their bounds of equipping students to one day carry out this societal change? Are students ever at fault for being too hasty to be activists? What are the ramifications of this hastiness?

3. In light of a tendency to disparage or ignore the past, what are strategic ways that you have found to lead educators and students to hold reverence for (learning from) the past? What classical literature, methodology, etc., work well to promote this?

4. Name an instance when you truly "threw yourself into the mind and heart of somebody who is not you." Did you find yourself feeling closer or more distant to this person in the aftermath? Are there instances when you developed a new friendship by doing this?

5. Corey describes how she changed majors in college and discovered the liberal arts. How did you choose your major in college? Do you think you made the right choice? Why or why not?

6. Mooney warns that doing a Ph.D. can feel like you are spending your time doing something useless. What does she mean? Is this feeling of uselessness something we are meant to overcome?

7. What does the concept of "total work" mean? Do you agree we live in a society that promotes a perpetual state of total work? If so, what practices can resist the mentality of total work?

8. Were you taught (formally or informally) to do "rage readings," that is, to read things for how wrong they are? Do you agree with Corey that this is a problem? Why? Have you had teachers how have helped you come to understand a reading even if they personally disagreed with it? How so?

9. Do Corey's warnings about the achievement culture and her endorsement of liberal arts education mean that she does not value a practical education?

REFERENCES

Flexner, Abraham. *The Usefulness of Useless Knowledge.* With a companion essay by Robert Dijkgraaf. Princeton: Princeton University Press, 2017.

American Academy of Arts & Sciences. *The Heart of the Matter: Around the Country.* Cambridge: 2016, at www.amacad.org/publication/heart-matter-around-country.

Augustine. *Confessions.* Translated by F. J. Sheed. Introduction by Peter Brown. Cambridge: Hackett Publishing, 2007.

Austriaco, Nicanor. "Identity Studies in Service of a Classical Education." *The Public Discourse,* February 15, 2017, at www.thepublicdiscourse.com/2017/02/18750/.

Brooks, David. *The Road to Character.* Large print edition. London: Random House, 2016.

Corey, Elizabeth. "Achievement and the Christian Life." *Faith and Public Life,* November 14, 2019, at www.faithandpubliclife.com/achievement-and-the-christian-life/.

Corey, Elizabeth. "Defending Disinterest." *National Affairs,* Spring 2018, at www.nationalaffairs.com/publications/detail/defending-disinterest.

Corey, Elizabeth. "Learning in Love." *First Things,* April 2014, at www.firstthings.com/article/2014/04/learning-in-love.

Corey, Elizabeth. "The University Has No Purpose." *The Chronicle of Higher Education,* April 22, 2018, at www.chronicle.com/article/the-university-has-no-purpose/.

Flexner, Abraham. *The Usefulness of Useless Knowledge*. Princeton: Princeton University Press, 2017.

Gombrich, E. H. *The Story of Art*. London: Phaidon Press, 1995.

Lewis, C. S. "Learning in War-Time." In *The Weight of Glory*. San Francisco: HarperOne, 1980.

Lukianoff, Greg, and Jonathan Haidt. *The Coddling of the American Mind: How Good Intentions and Bad Ideas Are Setting Up a Generation for Failure*. New York: Penguin Books, 2019.

Oakeshott, Michael. *Religion, Politics, and the Moral Life*. Edited by Timothy Fuller. New Haven: Yale University Press, 2011.

Plato. *Plato's Symposium*. Translated by Seth Benardete. Chicago: University of Chicago Press, 2001.

_______. *The Republic of Plato*. Translated by Allan Bloom. New York: Basic Books, 2016.

Virgil. *The Aeneid*. Translated by Robert Fagles. New York: Penguin, 2010.

ADDITIONAL READINGS

Corey, Elizabeth. "Against Campus Activism." *Real Clear Policy*, August 2, 2019, at www.realclearpolicy.com/articles/2019/08/02/against_campus_activism_111250.html.

Corey, Elizabeth. "Notes on Summer Camp." *First Things*, December 2019, at www.firstthings.com/article/2019/12/notes-on-summer-camp.

Deresiewicz, William. *Excellent Sheep: The Miseducation of the American Elite and the Way to a Meaningful Life*. New York: Free Press, 2015.

Halfacre, Philip D. *Genuine Friendship: The Foundation for All Personal Relationships, Including Marriage and the Relationship with God.* Woodridge: Midwest Theological Forum, 2008.

Lewis, C. S. *The Four Loves.* London: Collins, 2012.

Mooney, Margarita. "All the Single Ladies, Married Men, And… Everyone Else: Resisting the Mentality of 'Total Work.'" *The Public Discourse,* May 8, 2014, at www.thepublicdiscourse.com/2014/05/13092/.

Mooney, Margarita. "Fighting the Burnout Culture: How Personalist Philosophers and Benedictine Monks Can Help Stressed-Out College Students." *The Public Discourse,* August 28, 2018, www.thepublicdiscourse.com/2018/08/39415/.

Mooney, Margarita. "Happiness at Yale." *The Public Discourse,* September 16, 2014, at www.thepublicdiscourse.com/2014/09/13763/.

Postman, Neil, and Andrew Postman. *Amusing Ourselves to Death: Public Discourse in the Age of Show Business.* New York: Penguin Books, 2005.

Timothy P. O'Malley, Ph.D., is the director of education at the McGrath Institute for Church Life, University of Notre Dame. He is also the academic director of the Notre Dame Center for Liturgy, and a concurrent faculty member in the Department of Theology at Notre Dame. He teaches and researches in areas related to liturgy, Catholic education, aesthetics, and marriage and the family. He is the author of six books and editor of the forthcoming *The Liturgical Orientation of Education*. He is married to Kara and has two young children.

CHAPTER 4

Experiential Education: Comparing John Dewey and Luigi Giussani

Timothy P. O'Malley *and* Margarita A. Mooney

Mooney: Tell us about your own education and, specifically, how you came to study John Dewey.

O'Malley: I grew up in Maryville, Tennessee. I went to the University of Notre Dame for my bachelor's degree in theology and philosophy, where I grew very interested in liturgical studies. My senior year, I happened upon Jean LeClercq's *The Love of Learning and the Desire for God* (1960). Its central insight would guide my scholarship going forward: that there is a connection between prayer and the life of worship, and that there is a connection between learning and the desire to know. I did a master's degree in liturgical studies at Notre Dame focusing on this. Along the way, I came to realize that the thing that interests me was the interrelationship between educational theory—what it means to learn—and theology.

To continue this line of study, I pursued a doctorate at Boston College, where I encountered John Dewey's writings for the first time. He was involved in starting the Religious Education Association, and he argued for a broader inclusion of religious education in public life. I was very sympathetic to his argument that education is not simply throwing content into the head of the student; it has to have something to do with real life.

At the same time, I had problems with Dewey's understanding of metaphysics, of the human person, of his own conception of religion as a whole. I often found him as an interlocutor that I had to deal with. I did my work on Saint Augustine as offering a distinctive model of education grounded in worship in a way radically different from Dewey.

Eventually, when I returned to Notre Dame as a professor, I began to teach theology and education for undergraduate and graduate students. In this work I return again, in essence, to wrestling with Dewey's proper diagnosis but improper prescription.

MOONEY: Dewey is most known for the idea of experiential education. What is it, and why is it so significant?

O'MALLEY: Experiential education for Dewey comes from the idea that human beings learn best by actually working and engaging in the world—experimenting in and experiencing it. The world presents you with problems and you solve them. In an education setting, a teacher sets up a classroom as a space that allows people to experiment rather than simply to receive information. Now, a person needs some knowledge, some basic understanding in order to problem-solve, but the goal is not the knowledge but the solving of the problem. The scientific method is integral to this.

Dewey rejects a traditionalism in which ideas are merely passed on for no reason, or a traditionalism that reserves these ideas exclusively for an elite, where the thinking goes, "If you're an elite person, you deserve to know this. But if you are to work in a factory, you don't, so why worry about it?"

Dewey's experiential education is often misunderstood. Many people stereotypically envision a school in the luscious hills of Vermont where people are given a guitar and a rock and they figure out together how to understand music and count and eventually develop calculus. That is not Dewey's idea of experiential education. Education is neither just passing on a body of knowledge nor a sudden explosion that happens if you just put the right things in place. The teacher should be trained to educate on purpose rather than by accident, and to set up the right environment for the sake of learning.

MOONEY: So, one might say that Dewey was reacting to a version of a traditional education that was pure rote memorization, trying to strike a middle ground between this ridiculous image of giving kids a guitar and a rock and a rigid traditionalist education. His version of experiential education was different than other people at his time, people who didn't actually think that teachers mattered and who didn't think that content really mattered. Dewey's experiential education was trying to emphasize how people learn through experimenting, or by practicing things.

In *Education at the Crossroads* (1942), Jacques Maritain says that there is a lot to be admired in this version of experiential education, but that there's a deeper problem in how often it is framed.

What does Dewey say about the role of religion in education, for example?

O'MALLEY: There's an irony in Dewey's own religious background. He grew up as a Congregationalist in Vermont. As a young adult, he took on a religious vision informed by Hegel, studying with Hegelian philosophers at the University of Vermont and later at Johns Hopkins University in Baltimore.

Hegel was a philosopher who draws from a conception of a Christianity that moves beyond the particulars of doctrine to the level of statements of truth. Take the resurrection of Jesus. For Hegel it is a non-historical reality—Christ himself did not rise, but the principle that all of life shall be redeemed is real. The supernatural element is dismissed, and what's left behind is a philosophy that adjudicates what's rational about the resurrection of Jesus. This then shapes what the church is: not the gathering of those who are interested in salvation, but the community that lives out these values.

Dewey's first job was at the University of Michigan in Ann Arbor, which had been formed as one of the first non-religious institutions for higher learning in the United States. Even so, the university wanted religious education to take place in the local parishes or congregations, and he served in that role. Later, when he moved to a philosophy position at the University of Chicago, in 1896 he founded an elementary school affiliated with the university that did workshops—the first such "laboratory school."

He left religion behind for years in his own thinking until he returned to it in *Art as Experience* and *Common Faith*, both published in 1934. In these works, the particulars of Christian faith were portrayed simply as a preparation for the faith of America, this faith in a democratic principle that if we all work together and engage in common inquiry, we can make a better world. For Dewey, this is what Christianity has always been leading to. Dogmatism and particular doctrines are to be left behind for what's authentic, which is this movement towards unity.

MOONEY: When Dewey talks about religion in *A Common Faith*, he says unequivocally that supernatural claims about religion, including doctrines and the creeds, are untrue, but that the values which arise from religion need to be preserved. This is something like the American creed of civil religion, a set of values that inspire us to live democratically and have faith in progress.

Where else were these ideas percolating?

O'Malley: Dewey's conception of religion, this reduction of religion to a democratic experiment, was fairly normative. The place it was most operative was in institutions of higher education that saw their entire mission as religious, whether they put forward any explicitly religious proposition at all or not. Colleges and universities commenced as religious entities that their students were invited to attend for "intentional religious instruction." Eventually, this changed, and the mission of simply teaching people to think or to understand or to participate in the democratic world became its own religious entity. It's a secular vision of the kingdom of God at hand.

In Dewey's relatively short essay "My Pedagogic Creed," he uses the kingdom of God precisely in this way. Rather than the Son of Man coming on a cloud of glory to judge the nations, the kingdom of God is to be sought exclusively where justice and peace reside. The kingdom is divorced from both Christ and the Church alike.

Dewey is not unique in putting forward the notion that religion teaches you to be contemplative, to pay attention to things, to be moral, and that as society that progresses, we no longer need the credal parts of religion. Religion had a role in the past. Religion has served its purpose and now we leave behind the religious institutions and the particulars of doctrine for the sake of what comes next. This view, of course, is the great temptation of modern philosophical interpretation of religious doctrine as a whole. The twentieth-century Catholic theologian Hans Urs von Balthasar called this the "cosmological reduction," where what is left of religion are the universal truths that would have been accessible to reason unto itself. Dewey follows that through to its end.

But of course, people still believe in religious creeds and doctrines, and not simply as illusions. That's a problem for Dewey.

MOONEY: Dewey tries to explain the persistence of these beliefs as a human psychological projection. If we were to know and apply his method of education and his view of democracy, we would no longer need to have supernatural beliefs in order to have values like justice and equality.

O'MALLEY: Right. Dewey was friends with William James, who argues in *The Varieties of Religious Experience* (1902) that a mystical thing can be "real," but its realness is psychological. It must be understood within a mode that is rationally acceptable. It cannot exist unto itself as a mystery to be encountered, as something that reason cannot fully grasp. They shared this pragmatism.

For Dewey, all thinking must operate within the dictates of the scientific method. But of course, anyone who has ever fallen in love, who has ever faced suffering or death or evil, knows that there are certain things in life that are not fully understood this way. When you're falling in love, you don't think, "Let's gather the data of this beloved person. Who is she? What is it that she offers for me? What is evident?" There's something more there.

The scientific method can show you the interrelationship between things that are perceivable, but for most of Western history, it was accepted that there are things that are not perceivable with the scientific method; things you cannot measure with the tools of that method.

MOONEY: Does Dewey see the human person having what we might call a soul?

O'MALLEY: No, at least not as Western tradition has determined it. Dewey continually rejects what he calls dualisms: body/soul, mind/matter. While rejecting this dualism has benefits, it also means that he eviscerates a good chunk of the interior life. Everything is lived in the exterior; our mind isn't an interior part of ourselves in any way, shape, or form. There's no soul or interior work of memory and imagination. All we are as humans gets reduced exclusively to interactions with the physical, tangible world.

There's no conception of the person as having an interior self—something distinct from our actions in the world. Dewey's philosophy reduces religion, social practice, and the memory of a society to nothing but dictates of rational memories that have been passed on from age to age.

MOONEY: So for Dewey, mystical experiences might happen but they're an aberration. They certainly don't lead you to anything that's true or good. Dewey tries to develop a view of human nature and the human good that excludes the soul and any kind of contemplation. This view of who we are is fundamentally different from that of thinkers like Jacques Maritain or Luigi Giussani, for whom it's a big mistake to negate the contemplative side of the person.

There's nothing wrong with experiential learning or problem-solving, but ultimately, pragmatist philosophy collapses anything about the transcendent, the relationship between a person to God, into an action in the world, into something practical. It's a subtle but really significant philosophical move to say that all we need to know about the person is in what the person *does* in the world.

TIMOTHY P. O'MALLEY *and* MARGARITA MOONEY

Luigi Giussani's book, *Risk of Education,* lays out a method of education that is both practical and open to the transcendent. Giussani's educational method includes dialogue and encountering the material world, but there are many words in Giussani that you don't often find in educational theory, like tradition and authority. And there is another really important word that is key to Giussani's method—the idea that the human person contains a mystery.

O'MALLEY: Reading Giussani was a revelation for me, but it came about nearly by accident. I was doing a directed reading on education and Christianity while teaching at Notre Dame. We read Augustine, Gregory of Nyssa, Thomas Aquinas, and Bonaventure. The students asked for something a bit more modern, and they proposed Luigi Giussani's *The Risk of Education.*

At last, I found in Giussani the conception of experience that responds to the needs of the human person in relation to the actual world. Education is a risk where one proposes to the student a hypothesis through one's life, through a tradition, and through an authority. Then you have to try to live that out. There is an experimental dimension to this, grounded in a community that lives a concrete form of life together.

After this, I began to read and teach all of Giussani's work, such as *The Religious Sense,* and his other writings. I found that it helped students training to be educators to think anew about a way of teaching—particularly one grounded in Christianity—for this day and age.

MOONEY: I also first read Giussani many years into my career as a professor. It was after finishing a three-year project on philosophy of social science. My formal training is in psychology and sociology. What I encountered in studying the philosophy and method of much of the social sciences was that most often, psychologists and sociologists don't want to talk about the soul, or transcendence, or mystery, or any kind of truth that couldn't ultimately be subjected to the scientific method or a cognitive process.

But can such a method capture all of human experience? Many people do have mystical experiences. I've met young adults who've never set foot in a church, who don't profess any creed, who still feel that they've experienced God in a mystical way. Why hold to a method that excludes the supernatural when that is not congruent with human experience?

In Giussani I rediscovered an idea of the human person as open to mystery, and as experiencing God in some direct way, what he calls the religious sense. Understanding human experience and how that relates to education must therefore include an openness to religious experience as a part of human experience.

In *The Risk of Education,* Giussani lays out a method of education that's very attuned to a holistic understanding of experience. What does Giussani mean when he talks about human experience?

O'Malley: Giussani doesn't think experience simply means what we undergo or what we do. Giussani is drawing from an extensive philosophical and theological tradition within Christianity holding that experience is the fullness of the human sensation; it is human life in all of the ways that it's lived. The human being is perpetually experiencing. It's the intellect, the thinking, the wondering, the imagining, and the reasoning—that whole range of what it means to be human. As Giussani writes in *The Religious Sense,* the tradition itself is already an experience, one that has been passed on across time and space. Experience is also a primordial experience, that initial encounter with the person of Jesus.

Experience has this richness that in Latin is called *sensio*, the sensation—not just any sensation, but one of wonderment, of understanding, of fullness. This is a deeper sense of experience than simply that which is undergone.

For Giussani, you have to approach experience and religion according to reason. There's a rational way of facing up to religion and then there is the task of appropriation of knowledge and faith, of taking something on for ourselves.

MOONEY: I want to highlight one thing that you just said: for Giussani, reason is something that helps us to understand all of reality. There's an objective truth to reality that's outside of our thinking about it or doing something in it. For Dewey, it's not clear that there's an objective truth outside of experience because nothing is given for Dewey.

The way Giussani uses reason critiques the modern temptation to make reason synonymous with the scientific method. Giussani makes the provocative claim that even the creeds of Christianity should be subject to human experience and rational verification in some way. But Giussani also says that human experience in and of itself has to be measured up against some kind of objective truth. To Giussani, attention to experience without some kind of philosophical system to order that experience is lacking something. Giussani would say that we need to test our experiences with tradition so that we can order our loves.

What does Giussani make of Hegel, who was such an inspiration to Dewey?

O'MALLEY: Although Giussani does not specifically write on Hegel, he was inspired by Hans Urs von Balthasar, a Catholic theologian who did have very direct critiques against Hegelianism. That said, if you think about the desire to reduce any religious tradition to something that is simply a kind of philosophical proposal—a rational thing—then the whole system of Giussani is a critique against Hegelianism. It's a critique against a desire for understanding religion as a series of universal principles that pass on through history again and again. For Giussani, a communion of friendship, love, and sharing concrete forms of life together is never reduced to an idea. It's incarnational at its very roots.

MOONEY: Even the way Giussani conveyed his ideas was incarnational. Instead of academic books on theology and philosophy, most of Giussani's writings have come through pastoral talks that he gave. Dewey sets up a false opposition between experience and tradition, while Giussani is trying to put them back together not just in theory but in practice.

Often, people who say they don't have a tradition or don't have a starting point sneak one in but don't put it out on the table and discuss it. This is why Giussani says we should take our traditions out of our "backpacks" and put them on the table to discuss them. When you deny you have a tradition, you can't examine it.

The world itself gives me the method to understand it if I'm attentive to it. That is very attractive when you think about the different ways of teaching in a classroom, whether you're teaching religion, philosophy, or science.

O'MALLEY: Exactly. Also, Giussani would say that the thing that I look at gives me the method I should use. Method isn't something I impose upon reality and employ universally. In fact, that over-rationalizes the world. Instead, the world itself gives me the method to understand it if I'm attentive to it. That is very attractive when you think about the different ways of teaching in a classroom, whether you're teaching religion, philosophy, or science.

MOONEY: It seems that the concepts of judgment and meaning are crucial aspects of experience for Giussani—you cannot even have an experience without making a judgment about the meaning of it. But for Dewey, the truth entails bracketing meaning because it's subjective. Only the scientific method is objective. Is that correct?

O'MALLEY: I don't think Dewey would consider anything to be subjective, because he doesn't think there's a pure subject. Something is true insofar as it allows you to advance and to solve the problem, because it works or doesn't work. Dewey did acknowledge early in his career that the scriptures were true, but the truth of them is that they allowed a community to gather around a central idea and move forward. However, the particular truth claims were not valid.

For Dewey, the true thing is what allows the experiment to continue. It's then added to the body of knowledge so that you can advance knowledge from there.

MOONEY: Dewey uses words like subjective or subjectivity, but what he means by them philosophically is unclear because everything that's subjective has to be done in action. For Dewey, knowledge is an instrument: there's a problem to be solved and you fix it. In Dewey's framework, there's never a place for pure awe or contemplation because all of knowledge is instrumental.

Giussani thinks that there is an objective quality to who we are as human persons *and* to the meanings that we create in the world. Love and joy are not instruments; experiences of love and joy tell us something fundamentally true about who we are as human beings. Those experiences tell us something true but we didn't get there through the scientific method. That's why Giussani wants to point us back to understanding the fullness of the human experience.

Giussani sees the search for truth as the adequation of the intellect, our ability to wonder, to imagine, to reason, to understand. There is an explosion of insight that comes with this energy, this excitement to see reality as it is.

This isn't easy to do. You can't just pass on these ideas to people without them examining them for themselves. The task of truth-seeking is the risk of discovery. Teachers have to give students the space to discover the truth.

O'MALLEY: Anyone who has taught literature knows that when you propose a book to be extraordinary—that it will transform your life—the risk of that task comes when the student actually has to think through the book with you. As a teacher, this goes for me as well: the risk that I have to engage in the same sort of encounter and measure myself against it. There's the risk of the encounter with the student, if he will take the question seriously. It's the risk of real encounter: your encounter with the concrete tradition that you propose, and that in that proposal you recognize that you learned something anew and that you have to judge yourself anew by it. Your students also do that for you. My students regularly challenge me. They offer the proposition back to me to reflect upon.

MOONEY: The risk to the student is that this method of education that Giussani proposes requires that the student be willing to make judgments but also to make a commitment to a particular way of life. The end of this journey for Giussani is not eternal doubt, as it is for Dewey. It's certainty, and certainty requires a kind of existential commitment.

Dewey claims that there is really no end goal for education beyond growth. The aim of growth is to be able to grow more. What are the consequences for students who think of growth and learning as its own end, rather than growth towards God?

O'MALLEY: For Dewey, growth is for its own sake. To have no *telos* means that the person is just developing. There's an undercurrent of evolutionary theory to Dewey in that the human person is this incomplete entity that is ever evolving towards greater and greater levels of development.

This, of course, is very different from a Christian sense of the human person being made for happiness in its fullest sense. This is the beatific vision: to see God face to face. Ultimately, Christian education is directed toward that end—a particular end, rather than aimless, indeterminate growth. There's a reason that we read these texts or these ideas or encounter these doctrines. Not because we're just growing generally but we're growing towards union with God. That's not to say that, "Well, since I'm growing my *telos* towards God then I only need to know these eight things and then I'm done." It actually makes the goal of education even larger.

Reading Augustine offers an alternative model. Where are you at the end of Augustine's *Confessions*? Where you were at the beginning, which is asking who God is. The act of questioning, that desiring, that searching is part of the knowing. You can't know it in the way that you know other things. What you're left with is praise. If the human person is a liturgical creature, a creature made for worship, made ultimately to give himself away in love to God who is love, then that changes everything. It changes what's proposed. It even changes what a successful education looks like.

Mooney: When I was on the faculty at Yale and living in an undergraduate dorm and reading books with students on happiness, I discovered that a lot of students wanted to talk about something other than growth for growth's sake. They had implicitly felt, as I once did, that what made them valuable as a person was always achieving something more. They sensed there's something not quite right there, as everyone has limitations. We all have failings. Some might experience mental illness. In my experience, young people are looking for a psychology or an anthropology that's deeper than one that says you can perfect yourself, since that sets them up to feel like a failure when they encounter limitations to what they can do.

Education is not fundamentally a competition. The life of the mind is supposed to be intrinsically joyful.

If the human person is a liturgical creature, a creature made for worship, made ultimately to give himself away in love to God who is love, then that changes everything. It changes what's proposed. It even changes what a successful education looks like.

I often wonder if the modern rise in Buddhist meditation, mindfulness, and depth psychology indicates a hunger for something spiritual that has been lost. Do you think mindfulness fits in with Dewey's vision of religiosity and education, which focuses on behaviors and values without the creedal foundation to religious doctrine? What do you think about mindfulness used in Catholic education?

O'Malley: I've often found in educational literature a real interest in Eastern approaches to mindfulness because it is perceived to be devoid of doctrine. The goal is to empty yourself of any particular beliefs. In some ways, the desire for mindfulness is the desire to break out of a world and enter into a classroom that is sheer activity.

My critique of mindfulness in Catholic schools is that there actually is a richer tradition of contemplative life that we could draw from that is as integral to this as any sort of mindfulness conversation. This is where I turn to Leclercq's book *The Love of Learning and the Desire for God*, which states that knowing is a matter of contemplation, of attending, even of rejoicing or praise.

Why couldn't a Catholic school draw on that tradition instead? Couldn't a Catholic school be particular in its proposal rather than reductive? Catholic schools teach generic mindfulness because they actually don't know their own tradition well enough in its particularities. The temptation is to reduce the tradition to these universals, to rationalize the practice of contemplation. I would prefer that Catholic schools retrieve the real traditions so that we engage in authentic dialogue with those who are different than us. This allows us then to say things like, "Well, that is in some ways different, but I'm grateful that there is a commonality and I recognize that the difference also matters."

MOONEY: In the appendix of his 2018 book *The Mindful Catholic*, Dr. Gregory Bottaro lays out the difference between Eastern mindfulness meditation and a Catholic view of contemplation. He says that when Catholics use the term mindfulness, it needs to be distinguished from Christian contemplation and prayer. He wants to retain the term mindfulness because he's trying to help Catholics—for example, those in the psychology profession or social work—to understand what mindfulness-based anxiety-reduction techniques are. He wants to keep mindfulness as a technique, not as a philosophy of the person. That's one way of thinking about it.

Mindfulness practices are responding to a real desire from students to recover contemplation—many students feel like their minds have been turned into machines or supercomputers. Being able to speak to them in the terms that they may have encountered is important for Catholic educators to be able to do. But, as you said, there's a rich literature on contemplation that the Catholic tradition can and should draw on. Being able to point out where Christian prayer is similar and different from mindfulness is important.

This twist on the meaning of religious practice away from particularities of certain traditions and away from truth claims is extremely important to understanding the ways that religion is talked about in United States today. Where do we see this way of thinking in the United States today?

O'Malley: A temptation that's endemic in Catholicism or in any religious group that claims that particularity is to simply reduce truth claims to what could be agreed upon by everyone. I suspect it's coming to an end because in some ways those who still care about religion care about specific truth claims, and they also know that they can dwell peaceably in a society with people who don't make the same claims that they do. That is actually a better model than pretending, for example, that the evangelical Christian and I, the Catholic, share everything in common. We don't, and we would have fundamental disagreements.

The goal isn't to reduce these truth claims, but to deal with the particularities of them. The former allows us to get along, but it also then turns religion into that which it's not. And thus, we're surprised, for example, that people believe religion enough that they do live their lives in a way that makes other people uncomfortable.

MOONEY: The idea that nothing about religion should make anyone uncomfortable in some ways can be seen as a legacy of Dewey's view of religion. People may not be aware of what an enduring impact Dewey had on education. Henry Edmondson's book, *John Dewey and the Decline of American Education* (2006), talks about Dewey's concept of human nature, his rejection of tradition, including religious tradition, and his rejection of metaphysics. These problems from Dewey persist in American education today, with its emphasis on novelty and innovation, and the lack of any real canon of texts. Many educational systems emphasize getting a certain type of grade, or getting a test score, or getting into the next program. The environment and curriculum became so constrained, all aiming at goals that could be expressed in numbers. Kids feel a lot of pressure to achieve, and they're losing the playful creativity and awe with which they were born.

One consequence of all this is an obsession with metrics and outcomes in education to the exclusion of anything transcendent. There is a poem by Michael Rosen:

> First they said they needed data
> about the children
> to find out what they're learning.
> Then they said they needed data
> about the children
> to make sure they are learning.
> Then the children only learnt
> what could be turned into data.
> Then the children became data.

For teachers who are working in this data-driven world, how do they bring fundamental questions back into education?

O'MALLEY: My reading of Giussani led to a conversion in me. I found myself wanting to foster an encounter alongside my students. True, there are still things to measure. I need to know that they actually read the book. Still, I had to give up personally, as an educator, the embarrassment that comes in acknowledging that people take your class because it helps their lives. You feel bad because people take your class because they get something meaningful out of it, rather than that it's hard and prepares them for graduate school. I had to get over that.

MOONEY: I love your idea of thinking of teacher-student interactions in classroom as an encounter. Educators who aspire to live up to this model of education we are talking about may feel like they are swimming against the stream of their own educational institutions, but they can have a tremendous impact on students.

To demonstrate the impact of this approach to education, in addition to all the survey-based quantitative assessments that my students have to do, I have them write a qualitative evaluation of my class. I ask them to tell me one important thing that they learned, how that impacts their vocation and identity, and how they would describe this class to somebody else. I save these evaluations and use them when I describe the impact of my teaching to administrators. Administrators are moved by students' experience. If students praise your class and talk about how your teaching transformed their lives, administrators listen. I would encourage any educator to collect this qualitative kind of assessment alongside the quantitative measurements of student outcomes.

One thing I've learned from student feedback is that students really love the environment that we create together, which includes opportunities for play and humor. Humor (I sometimes even practice it intentionally) loosens up the brain. Our culture tends to think about the brain in a particular way, which reduces the human person to a thought-making supercomputer. Any thing that can loosen our brains again is so important because it helps spark our intrinsic human capacities for creativity, awe and wonder.

Giussani's method seems particularly applicable to people at the adolescent stage when students are coming alive to the elementary needs of the heart, when they hope to examine the proposal of a tradition. How might Giussani's method be helpful for preadolescent students when those questions aren't usually felt yet?

O'MALLEY: I think about this a lot because I have preadolescent children. In *The Risk of Education,* Giussani emphasizes that education doesn't begin only in school. The family offers a proposal for life from the beginning.

My seven-year-old doesn't ask, "Why do we pray every night before dinner? What is the purpose of that? What if I don't want to do it?" That's not where he is right now. Yet, what we do as a family is being offered as a proposal to him. In that sense, it's important to recognize the role of the family as passing on tradition.

As a father, I often think about what I am proposing to my child. What's my relationship with my smartphone? How much do I look at it? What proposition am I making about the meaning of life to my child on this? How distracted am I? How do I deal with punishment? Everything I do is inviting this child into a moment of coming upon what the meaning of life is. What hypothesis am I going to bestow? Where does my authority come from?

Right now, my authority comes from my kids because I am their dad. But one day, they're going to understand that there is authority which comes with their personhood. Do I live this out? The family is an integral dimension in the education of young children.

The school then has to be understood in relationship to that first dimension, which is that the family is proposing a way of life, and so is the school. That's sometimes where conflicts enter in. I think about what I want my son to *not* have in school; I want to avoid giving him the idea that his value or merit will be dependent on his academic success. If the school proposes that, I will fight the school. I have a particular role as a parent to fight against the credentialing, the logic of success ingrained in a method of learning that is grounded in our infinite desire to make our children into workers from the very beginning of their lives.

Mooney: Giussani was very influenced by the Benedictines. When it comes to elementary education, I have seen schools at the elementary level adopting aspects of the Benedictine poetic way of living. Children have an amazing sense of creativity and mystery. But children are also not resistant to memorizing things—they like to memorize poems and songs.

In a time like the COVID-19 pandemic when many students are learning from home, without experiencing things as they would on campus or at school, how can Giussani's concept of experience set their creativity free and enable education to continue in a different context?

O'Malley: It's easy to treat the COVID-19 pandemic as something to simply get through, to regret all that we're missing out on and wait for it to be over. Or we could treat it as a sign. For me, this period is raising questions about the kind of life that I was living. I was traveling all the time, very busy, always on the go. I never had space for just being. I didn't organize my life in the proper way. With this time away from students and coworkers, I find myself asking, "What is community like to me? What is my commitment to my neighborhood?" I've been really appreciative of Giussani teaching me not to focus exclusively on what comes after the pandemic, on how can I get beyond this. Instead, I use this moment as a sign that becomes educational for me.

MOONEY: In learning from home, we're not experiencing the kind of social world and the relationships that we normally are. But in addition to the tasks that I have to keep up with while working and teaching from home, I've been reading Dante's *Inferno* and Augustine's *Confessions*. There is a way that when you're reading some of these classical texts, you're experiencing in this original sense that Giussani is talking about. You're asking yourself these fundamental questions of human life. You experience awe and wonder reading great books.

In a time of crisis, we are compelled to consider who we are and what we desire. Reading classical sources while asking these questions is an incredible education that is available at any time.

DISCUSSION QUESTIONS

1. Do you think religion can be done away with if it has "served its purpose" of giving shape to a solidified democratic society? How does this play out in the college sphere as to whether or not particular institutions choose to sustain their religious foundations?

2. For educators: Name one instance of a risk that you took when offering something to your students.

3. For students: Name one instance of a risk that you took when trying out something your teacher offered you (i.e. a new concept, a different way of thinking, etc.).

4. Discuss O'Malley's statement: "Instead, the world itself gives me the method to understand it if I'm attentive to it." Do you agree? Do you disagree? Are there exceptions to this idea, especially for certain academic disciplines?

5. What are the sort of "existential commitments" that are most common to people and that assists them in their "certainty"? Which of these existential commitments are helpful to fostering discourse and understanding across different beliefs? Which are barriers?

6. Reflecting on your own faith tradition (if you have one), how has your tradition helped (or hindered) you order your deepest personal experiences?

7. How has your faith tradition helped (or hindered) how you experience contemplation, mindfulness, and/or an attentiveness to all of reality? Can you think of any particular educational experiences that helped (or hindered) how you experience contemplation, mindfulness, and/or an attentiveness to all of reality?

8. What literary works, especially pulling from the classics, have resonated with you during a time of personal difficulty or crisis? How so?

9. What is the difference in how Dewey and Giussani understand experiential education? Can you think of one example where this difference

might lead to a divergent way of teaching a particular topic like religion, literature, or science?

REFERENCES

Aquinas, Thomas. *The Academic Sermons*. Translated by Mark-Robin Hoogland. Washington, DC: The Catholic University of America Press, 2010.

Bottaro, Gregory. *The Mindful Catholic: Finding God One Moment at a Time*. Foreword by Peter Kreeft. North Palm Beach: Wellspring, 2018.

Deneen, Patrick. *Democratic Faith*. Princeton: Princeton University Press, 2014.

Dewey, John. *Democracy and Education: An Introduction to the Philosophy of Education*. New York: Macmillan, 1921.

Dewey, John. *Experience and Education*. New York: Free Press, 1997.

______. "My Pedagogic Creed." *School Journal*, Vol. 54, No. 3 (January 16, 1897): pp. 77–80, at infed.org/mobi/john-dewey-my-pedagogical-creed/.

______. *A Common Faith*. New Haven: Yale University Press, 2013.

Edmondson III, Henry T. *John Dewey & The Decline of American Education: How the Patron Saint of Schools Has Corrupted Teaching & Learning*. Wilmington: Intercollegiate Studies Institute, 2006.

Guissani, Luigi. *The Risk of Education: Discovering Our Ultimate Destiny*. Montreal: McGill-Queen's University Press, 2019.

James, William. *The Varieties of Religious Experience*. New York: Longmans, Green & Co., 1902.

Lopez, Antonio. "Growing Human: The Experience of God and of Man in the Work of Luigi Giussani." *Communio International Catholic Review*, 2010.

Newman, John Henry. *The Idea of a University Defined and Illustrated: In Nine Discourses Delivered to the Catholics of Dublin*. Chicago: Loyola University Press, 1927.

Nichols, O.P., Aidan. *The Word Has Been Abroad: A Guide Through Balthasar's Aesthetics*. Washington, DC: The Catholic University of America Press, 1998.

O'Regan, Cyril. "97 Theses on Hegel and His Catholic Readers." *Church Life Journal*, August 31, 2020, at churchlifejournal.nd.edu/articles/97-theses-on-hegel/.

Pope Benedict XVI. *A Reason Open to God: On Universities, Education, and Culture*. Edited by J. Steven Brown. Washington, DC: The Catholic University of America Press, 2013.

Redding, Paul. "Georg Wilhelm Friedrich Hegel." *The Stanford Encyclopedia of Philosophy*. Metaphysics Research Lab: Stanford University, Spring 2020, at plato.stanford.edu/archives/spr2020/entries/hegel/.

Saint Augustine. *Teaching Christianity*. Brooklyn: New City Press, 1995.

ADDITIONAL READINGS

Gioia, Dana. *The Catholic Writer Today: And Other Essays*. Belmont: Wiseblood, 2019.

Jacobs, Alan. *The Year of Our Lord 1943: Christian Humanism in an Age of Crisis*. New York: Oxford University Press, 2018.

Hildebrand, David. "John Dewey." *The Stanford Encyclopedia of Philosophy*. Metaphysics Research Lab: Stanford University, Winter 2018, at plato.stanford.edu/archives/win2018/entries/dewey/.

Marsden, George M. *The Outrageous Idea of Christian Scholarship*. New York: Oxford University Press, 1998.

Mooney, Margarita. "Newman's Vision of Liberal Arts Education." Margarita Mooney, May 7, 2018, at http://margaritamooney.com/2018/05/newmans-vision-of-liberal-arts-education/.

Mooney, Margarita. "Tradition and Authority in Luigi Giussani's Educational Method." *The Public Discourse*, April 15, 2019, at www.thepublicdiscourse.com/2019/04/50901/.

O'Malley, Timothy. "The Ideological Death of Catholic Education." *Church Life Journal*, August 12, 2019, at churchlifejournal.nd.edu/articles/the-ideological-death-of-catholic-education/.

Ratzinger, Joseph. *The Spirit of the Liturgy*. Commemorative edition, with *The Spirit of the Liturgy* by Romano Guardini. Ignatius Press: San Francisco, 2018.

≈

CARLO LANCELLOTTI is a Professor and the Chair in the Department of Mathematics of the College of Staten Island of the City University of New York (CUNY), and a faculty member in Physics at the CUNY Graduate Center. He is a Mathematical Physicist and specializes in the kinetic theory of plasmas and gravitating systems. He has also translated into English some of the works of Augusto Del Noce, a prominent mid-twentieth-century Italian philosopher and political thinker.

CHAPTER 5

St. Benedict and Education: Bringing Order Out of Chaos

CARLO LANCELLOTTI *and* MARGARITA A. MOONEY

MOONEY: Tell us about your own education. How did you come to know about St. Benedict?

LANCELLOTTI: It actually happened through my involvement in the movement of Communion and Liberation, which was started in Italy in 1954 by a priest named Luigi Giussani. His whole work and life were driven by the desire to communicate the Catholic faith. At first, Giussani taught theology at a Catholic seminary. But then he realized that many young people were not being properly catechized. So, he became a high school teacher to reach people for whom the culture and the tradition of Catholicism had been lost.

He was a high school teacher from 1954 to 1967. In 1968, amid a national crisis, all of the major Catholic student organizations in Italy fell apart. There was a big transition from a formerly hegemonic, Catholic culture to a situation in which Marxism became the prevalent magnet for young people, including many former Catholics and even many of Giussani's former students. The movement of faithful Catholic students that emerged from this was called Communion and Liberation, signaling the idea that true freedom or liberation comes through the Christian life. It was in this context that I, then a student, met him.

Giussani believed that one could not communicate Christianity to young people just by appealing to tradition, since tradition in many ways had been forgotten. To teach the faith anew, without presuppositions, he drew on the Benedictine emphasis on the elementary: the most fundamental, simplest aspects of Christianity.

MOONEY: What is this Benedictine understanding of the elementary elements of Christianity?

LANCELLOTTI: The way Giussani understood it, Benedict's charism was a "charism of beginning" because it identified Christianity in its most elemental or elementary aspects: simply, the reality of the body of Christ. Christianity appears in the world as a new human phenomenon, the community of the Church— not just the Church as an institution. The Church is primarily a communion of people.

The most elementary aspect of Christianity is not its theology. The long history of Christianity has produced many sophisticated cultural expressions: art, music, many different spiritualities, ways of praying, and ways of thinking. But to Giussani, the most elementary aspect was simply the appearance of a human phenomenon. In the most elementary sense, Christ left behind a group of people.

MOONEY: You have said that instituting order out of chaos is the witness of the life of the body of Christ. What did you mean by this?

LANCELLOTTI: The *Rule* of St. Benedict is meant to be practiced by normal people living in community. You pursue some kind of service, but your service is really your way of life, the people you live with and the way you work. The *Rule* of Benedict is organic—it can absorb every aspect of life: work, the liturgy, eating together. Everything is part of this communal life, and so the Benedictine idea is cooperative and social. As the British historian Christopher Dawson has said in his book *The Making of Europe* (1936), the Benedictine idea was not to produce heroic feats of asceticism but the cultivation of the common life.

True social order cannot be imposed top-down. Sometimes, people expect that there is going to be a politician who is coming in to impose order. That's a misunderstanding because real order comes from the bottom up.

The common life means more than just praying together, but prayers are the foundation of common life. And all of life becomes a form of prayer. The two things—life and prayer—are the same phenomenon that expands. As it expands, it takes in the cares of society around the monastery.

I grew up in Milan, Italy, where it used to be the case that if you went out of the city in any direction, there would be a Cistercian monastery, a branch of Benedictines. At one point there were as many as eighteen Cistercian monasteries around the city, with little else. The whole region used to be swamps and forests, until in the twelfth century the Benedictines (Cistercians) came along and drained the swamps, cut the forest, planted crops, and turned the area into a breadbasket. This order that was imposed on the land shows, in a sense, how civilization restarted out of complete disintegration.

But this order was not imposed extrinsically; it was the expansion of this life of the body of Christ, a meaningful society with an organic belonging. It's not just a spiritual belonging.

MOONEY: Some have said that the law of God is written on the heart, not simply enforced by moral codes or anything that takes away our free will. A Christian might understand living accordingly as abiding in Christ. Is this what it means to bring order out of chaos in one's own life?

LANCELLOTTI: Abiding in Christ cannot be solely interior or individual. Certainly, we experience Christ personally. But the communal and social aspects are fundamental to the Benedictine charism. Benedictines created order by building this network of relationships, because in these relationships it was possible to meet and follow Christ. The objectivity of the experience of Christ comes through encounters with the human reality that Christ left behind, with the body of the church.

This was the big change the *Rule* of St. Benedict brought to the monastic tradition. St. Anthony and the other Desert Fathers were hermits. Their vocation was not communitarian. By contrast, the Benedictine tradition emphasizes that we know Christ through his body, the human reality of the church. The monastery is a small image of the universal church. We live life not as individuals, but in communion.

In his *Rule,* St. Benedict talks about the four types of monks: the cenobites, who live together in a monastery according to a rule; the hermits, who live alone after their training; the sarabaites, who live in groups of one to three with no structure; and the land lovers, who travel from one monastery to the next. Benedict does not take a rosy view of sarabaites roaming around or land lovers living the good life, using other people's monasteries as a base. Although the hermits had more discipline, in his *Rule* he seems to think that they were a little bit too much. You have to be very good to be a hermit, you have to be a kind of a superman.

But the way the cenobites live is possible for normal people. You are not there in the desert fighting the devil all by yourself, facing many temptations alone. No, you are in a place where you are supported by a community, by the body of Christ. This is the purpose of Benedictine stability. It seems to be moderate and easy. But in reality, the stability is the result of a high degree of organization. However, the organization and stability are not ends in themselves but supports that make it possible for normal people to follow Christ in community.

MOONEY: Any of us could be a monk?

LANCELLOTTI: Well, for example you don't need to be a priest to be a Benedictine. The sacrament of baptism incorporates us in the body of Christ. And this very factor, being incorporated in the body of Christ, is all you need to be a monk.

The Benedictine tradition has a very strong sense of the church's *corpus verum*, true body. In a famous book titled *Corpus Mysticum* (2006), Henri De Lubac pointed out that many Catholic theologians in the first millennium (Rabanus Maurus, for example) routinely used *corpus verum* to describe the church, and *corpus mysticum*, mystical body, to describe the Eucharist. This was the understanding at the time of Benedict, but over the next millennium these two things got turned around.

To emphasize the Blessed Sacrament, people began to say that the Eucharist is the true body. And then the church became the mystical body as it is described in recent theology. In a sense, Giussani re-emphasized the older understanding. Of course, the sacraments and liturgy are essential, but they are *ecclesial* realities. The sacraments build and sustain the body of Christ, and the liturgy is the prototype of the absorption of every aspect of creation (the bread and the wine, the words and the gestures) into the life of that same body.

But the thing to remember is that Christianity started because people met a man. Peter and Paul and John and James and the other apostles met a man. Before all the understanding of who that man was, the theological reflection, the development of the liturgy, there was the elementary fact of the human reality of Christ. And by analogy the human reality of the church, the human community of the monastery itself.

MOONEY: The *Rule* of St. Benedict presents a way to live together in community and to praise God together—thus called a charism, or spiritual gift. When I was teaching at Yale, a group of students and I drove to Regina Laudis, a Benedictine abbey in Connecticut, where I came to truly appreciate how the Benedictine tradition is meant to be learned by experiencing it. I saw firsthand how the Benedictine way of life orders every aspect of the day towards contemplation—work, prayer, and common meals. I was astounded by how entering this beautiful monastery allowed me and my students to feel this organic unity. Our experience bonded our group together in a very palpable way. The Benedictine commitment to hospitality and welcoming the stranger is a way of life that spreads simply by sharing in its simplicity.

In fact, I named my nonprofit Scala (Latin for *ladder*) because I was inspired by St. Benedict's use of image of the ladder in Chapter 7 of the *Rule* to symbolize the balance between body and soul. The steps of the ladder represent that we ascend to excellence while also descending in humility. A ladder also symbolizes that being well-rooted in community life holds us steady as we climb to contemplate eternal truths.

One challenge in education today is that young people are suffering from a crisis of attention and a lack of imagination. Not educating the inner core of our soul from which all other capacities emanate—including our reason—has led to dissonance, dispersion, and the fragmentation caused by a lack of direction for our drives, passions, and instincts.

Climbing the ladder illustrates the idea that, as we strive for excellence, we continuously find ourselves on the bottom rung. I have experienced this as a hardworking person spending most of my adult life as a student or professor in the Ivy League; I feel like I'm always starting over every day on the bottom rung of a ladder. Like you said, the Benedictine charism is about beginning anew—the idea that the way to greatness is to start again every day with small acts is very encouraging to me.

The Benedictine tradition can still flourish in modern society in a variety of ways. Some new classical schools are drawing on St. Benedict, such as St. Benedict's Classical Academy in Natick, Massachusetts, run by lay people. There's St. Benedict's Preparatory School in Newark, New Jersey, that works mostly with African Americans and is run by the Newark Abbey of Benedictine monks with may lay teachers as well.

Why the renewed interest in the Benedictine way of life today?

Lancellotti: If you look at church history, the Benedictine story keeps restarting—for the first time during the Roman Empire, then at various stages of European Christianity, then again after the French Revolution when many monasteries were destroyed, and once again today.

Many people perceive a crisis, sensing that society is fragmented and civilization is declining. Many are asking: Is disorder growing in society? If so, what do we do? It's not by chance there has been a successful book called *The Benedict Option*, by Rod Dreher (2017). The desire many feel is to find some footing, some solid ground on which to build common life in modernity. This intuition is important and we should strive to understand it.

But people often misunderstand the so-called Benedict Option in the same way they misunderstand the Benedictine tradition, thinking of the Benedictine way as a retrenchment: that with the world falling apart,

St. Benedict retreated, going back out of society to a defensive posture in which it was possible to protect something. Now, in my understanding, this is not the point of the Benedictine way. Benedict's point was not a defensive posture or entrenchment, but a return to essential, elementary Christianity. Where, as I said before, elementary does not mean *easy* but *elemental*—the fundamental elements of Christianity that even somebody who is completely new can understand and live.

Benedict's point was not a defensive posture or entrenchment, but a return to essential, elementary Christianity. Where, as I said before, elementary does not mean easy but elemental—the fundamental elements of Christianity that even somebody who is completely new can understand and live.

A proper understanding of the Benedict Option, as I see it and try to live it, is more a matter of recovering the roots of Christianity in order to recover the possibility of life as a body of Christ, of life in communion.

MOONEY: John Henry Newman said that what really makes the Benedictine charism special is what he calls poetry. This term—or what Jacques Maritain calls poetic knowledge—means understanding the creative intuition that emanates from the soul of a person. It is a kind of preconscious activity that expresses itself in a work. Newman and Maritain talk about a creative intuition of the soul that expresses itself, works itself out through the practical intellect into something like a painting or a poem, but also may be expressed through the labor of working the land, craftsmanship, and cooking.

What do you think this idea of Benedictine charism as poetry means?

LANCELLOTTI: Newman writes of poetry as a form of knowledge, one which is essentially symbolic. It's not grasped primarily through intellectual elaboration. It's not that the Benedictines do not value reason, but they do not consider it the highest priority. Think of a toolbox of life from which you can choose different tools. St. Benedict chose to use the tool of intuition through symbols: through the gestures of common life including work, if you think of agriculture, the cycle of the seasons, or the cycle of life in the community as being laden with symbolic meanings.

Benedictines have a deep awareness and consideration for the harvest, meals together, and the sacraments. In a way, these things prefigure heaven. They require a discipline of attention—to nature, to community life, to the balance and the cycle and the meaning of the actions of daily life. To live in a poetic way means to perceive the symbolic dimension of experience. This is something that everybody can do.

One can use the tool of theology, too. But again, if we are talking about something that is accessible to everyone, certainly a poetic method is more practical. Think of ancient peoples and cultures: at the beginning of civilization, culture was expressed through epic tales like in Virgil or Homer. An epic poem was the soul of a people; it united people in a common awareness. Philosophy is a later fruit of intellectual and cultural life.

MOONEY: The discipline of attention, being present in the moment, is a major challenge in modern life. One way that Benedictines seem to encourage attention to the present is through craft and small aspects of manual labor, and avoiding too much technology. What else does the Benedictine charism teach us about how to develop greater attention?

LANCELLOTTI: I'm not aware that St. Benedict himself wrote about attention in those terms. However, I think attention is a habit that has to be cultivated. As Simone Weil has written in her book *Gravity and Grace* (1952), attention is the fundamental human faculty. In fact, she said that attention is prayer and prayer is attention. Like many things, habits are developed, but the habit of attention is the human response to God.

I would note that the human faculty for attention takes priority over creating new things. Our epoch puts a big emphasis on human creativity, the idea that human beings can be creators. That's true because in some sense we are meant to be co-creators with God. However, our creativity is secondary. Our fundamental posture should be one of attention, which is prayer.

Our epoch has a big emphasis on human creativity, the idea that human beings can be creators. That's true because in some sense we are meant to be co-creators with God. However, our creativity is secondary. Our fundamental posture should be one of attention, which is prayer.

MOONEY: How can we understand leisure time in our daily lives, and how is leisure related to the Benedictine emphasis on cultivating creativity and seeing human nature in an organic, even ecological sense?

LANCELLOTTI: Giussani used to say that leisure time is when we discover what we really care about. Leisure time is when you find out what you would do with all of your life if you could, right? When we have leisure time, we must resist the temptation to just unwind. Instead, we must ask the question: What do I really want? What is it I really care about?

Leisure time is going to be where activities we value as ends in and of themselves are pursued.

MOONEY: Singing is a wonderful expression of leisure. One of my more poignant memories of being at Ampleforth Abbey in the United Kingdom for a Scala seminar was when a student started singing the *Salve Regina* in Latin in the main church. I started singing with her, and then another person joined in, and then later the whole group joined. It was creative and organic. Suddenly, every day, the group of students began to sing together and it strengthened the bonds in our community.

This way of including singing in education seems to be at odds with a pragmatist view of education, where the emphasis is on analysis, inputs, and outputs.

Do you think education has become too focused on pragmatic ends?

LANCELLOTTI: First of all, education should also help develop our attention. As I said before, the poetic faculty means to be able to be mindful of the symbolic sacramental aspects of life, to see that things are beautiful. People must be attracted to the beauty of the world in order to study it. If the world was not beautiful, we would not be interested in finding out the laws of physics or other fields of science. In their book from *Galileo to Gell-Mann* (2009), Marco Bersanelli and Mario Gargantini created an anthology of around one hundred famous scientists like Marie Curie and Albert Einstein, describing how beauty and awe motivated their scientific discoveries. Speaking as a physicist and mathematician myself, I'm not surprised to read that the great physicists and the great mathematicians always loved what they did because of the beauty that they discovered in the world.

In my opinion, the real scourge of education today is utilitarianism, the sense that its primary goal is, essentially, to prepare for a career. Of course, getting a job is important. You need to make a living. But ultimately, if you narrow the goal of education to such limited usefulness, nobody would try anything new. In order to risk, to explore different fields, to do something that may not work, to do something that may not produce an immediate return, you need to have a bigger desire.

Even to introduce young people to the sphere of work in the utilitarian sense, you need to introduce them to a broader sphere of education. A passion for every aspect of life may come by way of art, poetry, history, or literature. If you have this kind of general passion for reality, then you are going to be able to focus on one part of it and really do a good job. But if you give up on the totality, if you are not attracted to life because life is interesting, and you just try to learn one skill, you probably are not going to do a very good job even with that one skill. Context is everything; we can't master one skill without the context given by other forms of knowledge.

One elemental human need is for meaning. Human beings ask the question of why. What is the meaning of this? Why do I have to study? Even young people, before they get brainwashed to focus on limited outcomes of some kind, they ask why: Why am I doing this? Modern education goes wrong when it alters its task from considering questions of meaning to seeing knowledge as a technique for problem-solving. This view of knowledge as problem-solving doesn't build up to a worldview.

A good educator must look at the students and realize that they are human beings, which means essentially religious beings. You have to give them reasons for what they are doing and what you are teaching.

MOONEY: In *Creative Intuition in Art and Poetry*, Jacques Maritain defines poetry as proceeding from the totality of the human person—this place where sense, imagination, intellect, love, desire all come together. Our modern culture has lost this understanding of the poetic dimension of the human person.

Newman wrote that the Benedictine charism presents a very elementary way of being a Christian in a world that lets each work, each place, each occurrence stands by itself. Being in each work, in each place as a totality in and of itself without having to necessarily conceptualize it, analyze it, and break it down into parts, is important. The Benedictine charism could be likened to the "being" mode of life and not the "analytical" mode of life that analyzes means and ends, looks at outcomes, or examines premises and conclusions. There's nothing wrong with any of that, but the Benedictine charism reminds us to also to be attentive to the total reality in which we are immersed at every moment.

Lancellotti: You are right. I think we could say that we live in a crisis of abstraction. We think that once we have analyzed things, that's all there is, that the idea is exhausted by our analysis. Everything gets filtered through some kind of pre-prepared abstract screen. Experience is replaced by our abstract explanations of experience.

What is really missing for so many today is the perception of beauty, of beauty as an opening to the mystery of God.

DISCUSSION QUESTIONS

1. Outside of the church, what other practices, communities, etc. help you carry out the Scala/Benedictine practice of the ladder—that we ascend to excellence while also descending in humility? Where do you think these kinds of practices should be emphasized more? Do you think

it *can* be practiced effectively in such an achievement-focused, competitive world?

2. Lancellotti talks about reclaiming the roots of Christianity in this day and age (engaging the world), rather than trying to subvert and/or flee from society (retrenching). In this time of constant innovation, digitalization, etc., what do you find to be perhaps the most difficult roots (elementary elements, as Lancellotti also describes them) to reclaim?

3. What have been the repercussions of a decline in attentiveness over the years for you personally? Society? What benefits would you and society more generally realize if cultivating attention became more of a valued habit?

4. In what ways has leisure time helped you gain insight into your passion and/or your vocation? How can our educational system better foster such structured leisure for the sake of discovering one's calling?

5. Can you think of an example that illustrates what Lancellotti calls the crisis of abstraction or what Mooney calls a crisis of imagination? How is the crisis of abstraction or imagination related to a loss of a sense of beauty or mystery?

6. Where do you see chaos today? How do you think education, Christian faith, and/or life in community can restore order?

7. Have you ever visited a monastery or an intentional community? What did you experience and/or learn that was applicable to your own life?

8. Reflect on your communities of faith throughout life. Have they changed? Have they grown stronger or weaker? Why do you think that is?

REFERENCES

Bersanelli, Marco, and Mario Gargantini. *From Galileo to Gell-Mann: The Wonder That Inspired the Greatest Scientists of All Time: In Their Own Words*. West Conshohocken: Templeton Press, 2009.

Dawson, Christopher. *The Making of Europe*. New York: Sheed & Ward, 1935.

Giussani, Luigi. *Christ, God's Companionship with Man*. Montreal: McGill-Queen's University Press, 2015.

_____. *The Risk of Education: Discovering Our Ultimate Destiny*. Montreal: McGill-Queen's University Press, 2019.

_____. *The Religious Sense*. Montreal: McGill-Queen's University Press, 1997.

Leclercq, Jean. *The Love of Learning and The Desire for God: A Study of Monastic Culture*. New York: Fordham University Press, 1982.

Maritain, Jacques. *Education at the Crossroads*. New Haven: Yale University Press, 1960.

_____. *Creative Intuition in Art and Poetry*. With an Introduction by Raymond Hain. Providence: Cluny Media, 2019.

Saint Benedict. *St. Benedict's Rule*. Edited by Patrick Barry. Mahwah: HiddenSpring, 2004.

Weil, Simone. *Gravity and Grace*. London: Routledge, 2002.

ADDITIONAL READINGS

Blum, Christopher, and Joshua Hochschild. *A Mind at Peace: Reclaiming an Ordered Soul in the Age of Distraction*. Manchester: Sophia Institute Press, 2017.

Del Noce, Augusto. *The Crisis of Modernity*. Translated by Carlo Lancellotti. Montreal: McGill-Queen's University Press, 2015.

Freire, Paulo. *Pedagogy of the Oppressed*. New York: Bloomsbury Academic, 2018.

Lancellotti, Carlo. "The Dead End of the Left?" *Commonweal Magazine*, March 21, 2019, at www.commonwealmagazine.org/dead-end-left.

Lopez, Antonio. "Growing Human: The Experience of God and of Man in the Work of Luigi Giussani." *Communio International Catholic Review*, 2010.

Mooney, Margarita. "Being Human in the Modern World: Why Personalism Matters for Education and Culture." *The Public Discourse*, June 25, 2018, at www.thepublicdiscourse.com/2018/06/21942/.

_____. "Lectio Divina and Online Learning." *First Things*, October 27, 2020, at www.firstthings.com/web-exclusives/2020/10/lectio-divina-and-online-learning.

_____. "Overcoming Flawed Educational Views of the Human Person." *Church Life Journal*, October 17, 2019, at churchlifejournal.nd.edu/articles/overcoming-flawed-educational views-of-the-human-person/.

_____. "The Love of Learning and the Lay Desire for God." *Church Life Journal*, November 6, 2019, at churchlifejournal.nd.edu/articles/the-love-of-learning-and-the-lay-desire-for god/.

_____. "The Poetic Body of the Benedictine Charism." *Church Life Journal*, October 16, 2020. churchlifejournal.nd.edu/articles/the-poetic-body-of-the-benedictine-charism/.

_____. "The Benedictine Charism as Poetry: Sacramental Living that Sows the Seeds of Order." In *A Benedictine Education: A Collection of Essays by St. John Henry Newman*. Edited by Christopher Fisher. Providence: Cluny Media, 2020.

_____. "Tradition and Authority in Luigi Giussani's Educational Method." *The Public Discourse*, April 15, 2019, at www.thepublicdiscourse.com/2019/04/50901/.

Pieper, Josef. *Leisure: The Basis of Culture*. San Francisco: Ignatius Press, 2009.

Sayers, Dorothy. *The Lost Tools of Learning*. Waterford: Crossreach Publications, 2017.

Tomaine, Jane. *St. Benedict's Toolbox: The Nuts and Bolts of Everyday Benedictine Living*. Harrisburg: Morehouse Publishing, 2005.

Waal, Esther de, and Kathleen Norris. *Seeking God: The Way of St. Benedict*. Collegeville: The Liturgical Press, 2001.

GEORGE HARNE is the Executive Dean for the School of Arts and Sciences at the University of St. Thomas in Houston. He is a scholar who holds a doctorate in musicology from Princeton University. His distinguished career in higher education encompasses his service as President of Magdalen College of the Liberal Arts (2011–2020), music professor, and teacher of the Humanities for over a decade. He is married and has five children. Dr. Harne engaged in this dialogue with Dr. Mooney while President of Magdalen College, where he further developed its curriculum and integrated humanities program.

CHAPTER 6

Liberal Education and Beauty

George Harne *and* Margarita A. Mooney

Mooney: Tell us about your education, and how you came to be a professor and president of Magdalen College of the Liberal Arts?

Harne: My journey began with playing and studying music. As an undergraduate, I played clarinet in the orchestra and the wind ensembles at the University of Southern Mississippi. Along the way, I discovered that I loved music history and began to focus on musicology. Then I made another turn, and I studied the Great Books at St. John's College in Annapolis, Maryland, which opened up a whole world of humanistic learning. After that, I completed my doctoral studies in musicology at Princeton University. I found myself integrating what I learned in studying the Great Books with what I studied in music. I was interested in bringing history, literature, and philosophy from the Great Books into a humanistic synthesis around big questions of human life, in particular around the fine arts and beauty.

I began at Magdalen College of the Liberal Arts as a professor in 2008, teaching the Great Books. At smaller liberal arts colleges like Magdalen, there is always a need for administrative service, and so a few years on

I stepped in as president. With wonderful memories of my time there, in the fall of 2020, I moved to Houston to be Dean of the University of St. Thomas's School of Arts and Sciences. But the long thread running through my educational journey is the love of music and its effect and impact on my life. Music shaped my world, my understanding of reality, and it gradually came to be my bridge to the humanities and philosophy.

MOONEY: I grew up in Frederick, Maryland, about an hour and a half from Annapolis, where St. John's College is located. I am sure you have heard the jokes about St. John's graduates, right? They are "the best-educated baristas you have ever met." I am sure people ask you all the time: What is my child going to do with a liberal arts degree that focuses on the Great Books?

Jokes aside, it's a serious question that I get asked all the time. As a proud graduate of St. John's and lover of music, how do you answer this question? What do the students in the schools where you have worked do with their education?

HARNE: At Magdalen, we read the classical texts and books, mostly in seminars, but we read them with the intent of coming to understand the truth of things in a holistic sense. We seek to become wise. This approach is different from my St. John's experience, where our seminars focused on a close reading of texts within a very limited horizon. While asking important questions like, "What do these books say?" and "What are the authors saying?"—we almost always stopped there, divorcing our reading from the larger questions about how we should live. At Magdalen, the perspective is more comprehensive and integrated across texts as well as being ordered to the acquisition of wisdom. We believe that there is a truth that is discoverable and knowable across texts. We spend four years with our students moving across the classic disciplines including literature, history and philosophy, from Homer to Heidegger and with many stops in between. We do this within the broader context of forming and educating the whole person. But beauty—liturgical beauty, the fine arts, and natural beauty—all play essential roles.

At Magdalen, as a Catholic college, we also have a lively liturgical and spiritual life, and students draw deeply from these, too, for their education. Someone said that our approach is almost like two lungs working together: one, the spiritual and liturgical life, and the other, the life of the classroom, which we approach as an almost-sacred space, set apart for the pursuit of wisdom.

But as human persons, we don't have only minds and hearts; we also have hands and feet. Our students engage in a wide variety of physical activities. One of our trustees generously built a greenhouse on campus, so students grow fresh food and fresh herbs and enjoy the fruits of their labor. The campus is on a mountain in New Hampshire, so students have a great time outside of class in nature hiking, skiing, and rowing. In some ways, it is a perfect life if you are eighteen. Mind, heart, and hands are fully integrated.

Across history, there have been different models of universities. There are the modern research universities that go back to the German model developed in the nineteenth century, and then there are the medieval universities of high scholasticism. But before high scholasticism there were smaller institutions that deeply integrated prayer and learning. Jean Leclercq, a Benedictine monk, discusses this earlier approach in his 1960 book *The Love of Learning and the Desire for God*. In many ways, our liberal arts college participates in the tradition Leclercq describes.

But all of this prepares Magdalen students to use their hands to cultivate what we call "the garden of the world." Each has been given a part of our world, our culture, our nation, and they are called to put their gifts in the service of the Church and the world. And they do. They lead lives of sacrifice, success, and fruitfulness born from their formation.

MOONEY: I often receive questions about what a liberal arts education is. The term liberal arts sometimes gets used to refer to slightly different models of education. One model is how you described St. John's College, where students read a curriculum of the Great Books of the humanities, philosophy, literature, etc. That is an excellent model of education. But liberal arts can also mean the classical trivium (grammar, logic, and rhetoric) and quadrivium (arithmetic, astronomy, music, and geometry)—where the aim is to introduce students to the primary forms of knowing. Some people use liberal arts to mean holistic Christian formation. Finally, others use the term "liberal arts education model" to emphasize the integration of beauty into learning, or the unity between the search for truth with the good and the beautiful.

How would you describe what a liberal arts education is? And how do you see the fine arts, or beauty more generally, as important to educating the whole person?

HARNE: When I talk about the liberal arts, I typically start with the trivium and quadrivium as Boethius (b. 480 AD), the sixth-century philosopher, understood them in order to get to this higher vision. Combined, the trivium and quadrivium provide an integrated sevenfold path that forms the mind, heart, and imagination while also introducing us to the basic structures of reality. But they fundamentally offer a path that takes us higher if we follow it. Taking an image from John Henry Newman, at Magdalen, we often explained the journey of liberal learning by saying that if you grew up in a town next to a mountain, you might know that town well—all of its details and textures—but then one day you may decide to climb the mountain. At its peak, after the arduous climb that is liberal learning, you will see the town you thought you knew, i.e., your reality, from a completely different viewpoint. The horizon is broad; you see other mountains and other towns in the distance and you see the town in which you grew up as an integrated whole, from a radically different perspective, and within a completely different context. That vision is as much of the whole as you can contain. And when you return to your town, your view of the truth of the place you thought you knew is completely different. The trivium and quadrivium—enlivened by poetry, music, and the other fine arts—are paths up the mountain where such a vision—the ultimate fruit of liberal learning—is possible.

I would also reach back further, to Aristotle. In his *Ethics,* he outlines three basic human activities: knowing, doing, and making. The liberal arts are rooted most deeply in the contemplative activity of knowing. The fine arts, in their acts of production, are born from the third activity, that is, making. But once they are made, they become the objects of contemplation, taking us back to the first category of contemplation, which Aristotle considered the highest human activity and one that participates in divine life. Thus, the fine arts tutor us in contemplation (as Josef Pieper suggested in *Leisure the Basis of Culture*), opening us to delight, joy, and love. The beauty of the fine arts can be a propaedeutic to the beatific vision.

Aristotle said that all men desire to know. You might then make the case that all men also desire to experience beauty, so it is also a fundamental human need. A liberal arts education that truly liberates us will integrate not only the trivium and quadrivium but also provide opportunities to experience beauty, perhaps even to make it.

Musical beauty, as a fine art, cuts across all three of Aristotle's categories of human activity: it is made, it is performed (an act of doing), and it is contemplated. As a mathematical art of the quadrivium as well, the beauty of music may be hidden, but it is no less real. It was this mathematical dimension, thanks to Boethius, that gave music pride of place in the Middle Ages as part of the quadrivium. Thus, music had dual citizenship as a fine art and a liberal art. The other fine arts did not enjoy this status and were relegated to secondary status until the Renaissance.

This brings us also to the idea that education should fundamentally be about formation or *paideia*: we are not merely acquiring facts but being formed by experiences inside and outside of the classroom. One of Heidegger's most important contributions was shifting the way we think about philosophy from being a purely academic discipline and retrieving an older tradition in which philosophy—understood as a life-informing pursuit of wisdom—should be something that shapes how we live our lives, including an encounter with beauty. The emphasis that philosophy places on fundamental questions opens a space for encountering beauty in new ways. This integrates philosophy, including the philosophy of art, with questions about the good life.

The best forms of liberal learning are about helping people to become fully human, and beauty is an essential part of that human development rooted in our anthropology, who we are as humans. This approach to education integrates the Great Books approach, Newman's approach, and the classical Boethian approach, which itself presupposes Plato's philosophy. The power of beauty cuts across all of these approaches.

MOONEY: Recently I have been reading and listening to Dana Gioia; he is a poet, a former businessperson, and former director of the National Endowment for the Arts. He did a powerful video for *First Things* magazine, in which, drawing on Thomas Aquinas, he described how beauty arrests our attention. Beauty leads us to take pleasure in what we are beholding in the moment and gives us glimpses of the inner workings of nature.

Further drawing on Aquinas, he described how beauty helps us to integrate the different parts of reality into a whole. If you've ever had an experience on a mountain or in a beautiful place of nature, where you feel this joy when suddenly all these different pieces of knowledge come together, and you can see the whole, it's an experience that gives clarity. Beauty radiates into our intelligence, deepening our knowledge of reality.

By contrast, many students tell me that their educational experiences are fragmenting. They are picking up pieces of knowledge, but they are not integrating all of the things that they are learning into a whole. I described how to respond to this fragmentation in *Church Life Journal*, in an article called "The Love of Learning and the Lay Desire for God," drawing on Jean Leclercq's book that you mentioned.

Could you say more about how beauty integrates different aspects of knowledge?

Harne: When you are getting to know a piece of classical music, you soon become very attentive to the relationships between parts and the whole, and the parts to each other. Take the sonata form, where you have the exposition, the development, and the recapitulation. You have themes developing, shifts in harmonic center, and wheels within wheels unfolding across time in a complex sonic architecture; any real understanding of such a work of music is going to require you to do an analysis and to bring those networks of parts and wholes to the surface. At a certain point, you return and create a "map" that is textured and multi-dimensional. Then you go back to listen to it anew as the piece of music unfolds through time but with a deeper understanding rooted in a comprehensive, yet non-reductive vision. Listening to a piece of classical music in this way involves a kind of teleological dance: each moment is significant while also being ordered to the whole and the work's ultimate resolution in time. This is an extraordinarily complex form of knowledge that engages the aesthetic sensibility as well as the listener's powers of memory, imagination, analysis, and synthesis.

Along the way, you developed habits of mind that are transferable to other parts of your life. Now, it is possible to study music in this way in isolation and not to let it affect the rest of your life. But at Magdalen, the work we do with texts, music, and art allows us to practice thinking teleologically, in terms of the parts and the whole. We then encourage students to think about their lives and their larger reality in those terms. What are the various parts of our lives? What is our *telos* as a human person—at what are we aiming?

MOONEY: The way you describe music education is inspiring. But when I was an undergraduate at Yale University, people were encouraged to take a class on music appreciation teasingly called "Clapping for Credit." Why might people jokingly call music appreciation classes by that name?

HARNE: At Princeton University, there was a class that students called the same thing. In fact, I taught the so-called "Clapping for Credit" course!

MOONEY: The joke points to the idea, I think that, anything goes in listening to music. Appreciating music is about experiencing pleasing emotions and expressing yourself by clapping. But how you described a music class in a liberal arts education is much deeper. How do you teach music the way you describe, unpacking the parts of a piece and then finding the *telos* of the whole?

Harne: The education does not occur only in the classroom. In the life of the student as a whole, education in music comes together in an integrated way. The first step is to learn to listen, to turn off the devices that vie for our attention, and to slow down the interior monologue long enough to deeply listen to music.

In some ways, the lack of music education is tragic. Imagine waiting to teach people to read until they get to college; you would never do that. No one would say we are going to learn the alphabet in week one, and then we are going to be reading Shakespeare by the end of the semester. And yet that is often the expectation in a music class in college. This is largely why "Clapping for Credit" becomes what it is—the students, intelligent as they are, are musically illiterate to start with, and it takes more than a single semester to bring them to a deep understanding.

Magdalen structures the curriculum to traverse this distance in music education. First, we teach students to listen, and we practice so that they learn the basic vocabulary of music. They learn to listen to various pieces—chant, polyphony, Baroque music, Romantic symphonies, twentieth-century music, and they become attuned to those musical structures. They explore them all in terms of parts and wholes, as well as teleological structures.

We also weave into the curriculum the philosophy of the fine arts, so they read Étienne Gilson, Jacques Maritain, Walter Benjamin—people who have reflected on art from an aesthetic perspective, its reception, making, and the philosophy of art.

Listening this way helps us recover the classical vision of the human person that integrates body, mind, and spirit. Today there is a temptation to fall into a reductive dualism in which our bodies are mere tools and our true selves are our minds, or our complete personhood is reduced to the materiality of our bodies. But we cannot see and hear beauty without our physical senses, yet we remain on the surface of things if our mind and spirit do not take up this physical experience of music and its depth of sound.

So, Magdalen's students don't just listen; they also sing polyphony, they perform chant and other works in a liturgical context. Their bodies physically experience what it's like to sing one line, while the person next to them is singing another. If they are on tour, there is an audience present; the audience is smiling and appreciating it. But there is also a sense that the music is ordered to a higher end that transcends the aesthetic itself, and that music is more than just the pleasurable sensations one might feel at a moment in time.

So, studying music is more than a class—studying music helps order an integrative education. When I was studying musicology at Princeton University, I did not have this vision; it took years for me to develop it as I learned from my colleagues and my students. It is a beautiful way to educate people. I receive emails all the time from students after they have graduated; they miss the friendships but just as often talk about the liturgical life with specific reference to the music. Most of these people did not enter school as musicians, but they learned music deeply.

MOONEY: That's wonderful. Students are not just learning music in their heads, but feeling it and performing it. They learn that serious music education is also an education in philosophy. And the beauty of music is more than sensory pleasure, it is supposed to impact how we live.

How do fine arts and music complement the study of great liberal arts texts? Can experiencing beauty make us better readers and thinkers?

HARNE: Attentive seeing and listening we learn in music education as I've described them can activate our understanding and the experience of the dynamic relationship of parts and whole, resolution and irresolution, across various fields of knowledge. This kind of music education also trains the soul to think in terms of purpose. These same dynamics unfold in texts that constitute the studies of the liberal arts and help students develop wisdom by approaching the complexities of life. Just as the Great Books prepare us for human flourishing, so the experience of beauty and the fine arts can do the same.

Attentive seeing and listening we learn in music education as I've described them can activate our understanding and the experience of the dynamic relationship of parts and whole, resolution and irresolution, across various fields of knowledge. This kind of music education also trains the soul to think in terms of purpose.

MOONEY: Can the activity of making beauty make us better citizens?

HARNE: Our experiences contemplating and making beauty certainly can form us to be better citizens. These same dynamics present in the making of beauty can be thought of as skills and experiences that may be transferred—with guidance from political leaders and philosophers—into the political sphere. How much wiser would our citizens be if they came to understand more clearly the parts and wholes of our society, the places where things can be resolved and where they cannot.

Poetry also plays a significant role here, and I am indebted to Dr. Mary Mumbach, who is on the faculty at Magdalen College. I am only beginning to understand many of her insights. There is an irreducible dimension to poetry, as there is to life. We want students to recognize through liberal learning that sometimes you cannot cross all the t's and dot all the i's. There are parts of life that are irreducible in their complexity; the process of understanding life is always unfinished. Poetry can prepare us to encounter the mysterious in life, and it can inoculate us against certain ideologies that claim to explain and control everything.

MOONEY: Is the search for beauty important in fields that are not considered parts of the humanities?

HARNE: The four quadrivial arts are mathematical and scientific, fields that are fundamentally about thinking from presuppositions to conclusions. There is an immediate analogy between the structure of music (which, don't forget, is one of the subjects in the quadrivium) and the structure of art, math, and science. In both art and music, the whole is greater than the sum of its parts, but that is often true for scientific work and math as well. At the foundation of many of the fine arts, you will find an order, harmonious relationships, and a beauty that emerges from them; there is a fundamental *logos* behind it all. The same can be said for science and math.

MOONEY: I published a blog in *Scientific American* showing how a liberal arts education can help understand the whole person. We want the tools engineers make to reflect both good human ends and the symbolic dimension of the human person. Students in science and engineering often want an excellent liberal arts education, not just a purely technical education.

HARNE: The seven liberal arts are meant to cover most of reality. But they all need each other; no one can stand alone. There is a modern tendency for expertise in one discipline to claim preeminence over every other. John Henry Newman warned of what happens when you remove theology, for instance, from the curriculum. Certain subjects come rushing in to claim superiority over all other disciplines. Psychology, or heaven forbid, music history! We must remember to keep all of reality properly ordered and coherently organized toward a whole, to build to the truth; otherwise, knowledge becomes disorderly. Maybe that's why students tell you they have learned a lot of things but they can't integrate what they have learned. Without ordering principles, the pieces of knowledge we gain ultimately fall apart.

MOONEY: Many have lost the sense that there is a unity to all knowledge. Others have not even heard of the notion that beauty, art, literature, and poetry teach us something about truth. Many people across time have argued that beauty is purely subjective, and any meaning we give to it is a human creation, not a sign of an ordering principle about reality.

How would you respond to the notion that beauty and the fine arts are strictly subjective, whereas other fields of knowledge, in particular science and math, tell us something objective about reality?

HARNE: We owe our view of the arts as being almost exclusively subjective to the Romantics in the nineteenth century, when art and music could sometimes become a substitute for religion or metaphysics. Now, it's common, even among some artists or teachers of the arts, that the arts have no objective meaning—the fine arts are purely subjective, a matter of opinion or personal taste. At times, western culture has exalted the role of the artist to a near god-like status.

MOONEY: Is another objection to the idea that beauty is objective rooted in the idea that beauty can be misleading, as we get swept away irrationally by beauty, and therefore distracted from the search for the truth and the good life?

HARNE: That's an excellent question. When we consider the scholastic view of beauty in which there is a spark that catches our eye and completes the experience of beauty, that experience is going to ground us in the larger objective reality that undergirds it.

A more Romantic approach to beauty focuses on its subjective dimension. The Romantics of the nineteenth century shifted our understanding of culture to an extreme where musicians and artists have a purchase on reality that no one else has. The movement could be likened to an artistic gnosticism. The symphonies get larger and longer, and the egos are commensurate with the dimensions of the work. Artists are perceived to have a kind of insight—we see this in the French symbolists, who drew a lot from the poet Edgar Allan Poe, oddly enough, or in the Russian "World of Art." In a lot of the European aesthetic and poetic movements, the poet has supreme insight, insight we might not have.

Think of the three composers Bach (Baroque), Mozart (Classical), and Beethoven (Romantic). Bach was a church musician and taught children. He performed his many professional obligations to the glory of God, not for himself alone. Mozart was celebrated from an early age, but even so he took his meals next to the stable boy. By the time you have Beethoven, at the beginning of the Romantic period, he was an independent musical entrepreneur. He resisted any attempt to treat him the way that Mozart or Bach would have been treated—living in unity with manual laborers or children. By his late work, he is the quintessential example of the tormented artist.

Interestingly, the Romantic perception of some people having special insights into beauty in some ways harkens to an earlier tradition where people held that the poet Homer was inspired by the muses, and therefore had access to divine inspiration. This view goes far back in the Western tradition, and was quite strong in Romanticism. The view of the artist as a sort of heaven storming Promethius still endures today. It is the artist who stands outside of culture, who does the work of turning culture upside down and breaking things, which is an idea that is still present and part of us. If this is our understanding of art and the artist, it is not surprising that people are skeptical about the idea that art has an objective dimension or that it can lead us to truth or goodness.

MOONEY: How does this idea of beauty as subjective affect our understanding of integrated truth?

HARNE: We have to reclaim beauty and the arts from the Romantics and their heritage. Fundamentally, the arts are about order. Think of the classical definitions of beauty: unity, *harmonia*, the harmony of the parts to each other and the whole, and *claritas*—that gleam that catches the eye. The thing that attracts your attention and holds it—that is a piece of objective truth. Your response to it may be subjective, but it can lead—under the right conditions—directly to questions about the good and about the true.

This is why it is important to approach beauty not as an experience of consumption but as an experience of contemplation. One of the critical things that we can do to overcome the possibly deceptive dimension of beauty is to cultivate an attitude of listening and seeing that is fundamentally contemplative and open to the fullness of being. In *Leisure: The Basis of Culture* (1948) and the small book *Only the Lover Sings* (1990), Josef Pieper does an excellent job of showing readers this path.

Madgalen students practice that. Students attend concerts and visit museums in Boston and New York, where they can examine what they experience in the classroom and in their own performances while in those spaces. We approach these times as contemplative activities. We don't just walk through and glance at things and mention that this person did this or that. Experiencing concerts and museums is a much deeper contemplative activity which, of course, can be a preparation for the beatific vision. We are learning to see a work of art and listen to a piece of music as a foundation for something much more metaphysical. The best antidote to seeing beauty as consumption is to nourish the spark that we encounter in beauty within something more complete and more textured. Beauty is deceiving if fails to incorporate what we experience into the larger whole. Experiences of beauty need not stop in the moment something grabs our attention.

Fundamentally, the arts are about order. Think of the classical definitions of beauty: unity, harmonia, *the harmony of the parts to each other and the whole, and* claritas*—that gleam that catches the eye. The thing that attracts your attention and holds it—that is a piece of objective truth.*

MOONEY: Yes, beauty could be misleading when it becomes a form of consumption, or if we seek forms of entertainment that grab our attention superficially. Different forms of liturgy within Christianity sometimes touch on the difference between entertainment and beauty. Even Christian liturgy, which is supposed to be an experience of beauty that lifts our hearts to God, can sometimes feel soul-numbing, deadening, or downright misleading.

The McGrath Institute for Church Life at the University of Notre Dame has some excellent resources on the nexus between Christian liturgy and education. I also teach Roger Scruton's brief but deep book, *Beauty: A Short Introduction,* as a great resource for understanding the contours of the conversation around beauty, truth and the good life. Like you, he argues that beauty is objective and not subjective, and he describes the various reasons people differ on this question.

HARNE: The French philosopher Étienne Gilson offered a corrective against Romanticism in such books as *The Arts of the Beautiful* (1965) and *Forms and Substances in the Arts* (1966). He argued that art is unique and cannot be understood as metaphysics, politics, or ethics. To confuse these categories is to sow great confusion. They are related in important ways but deserve their own autonomy.

We can also look to Jacques Maritain's vision of the artist as a craftsman in *Art and Scholasticism,* where he challenges us to rethink the role of the artist as doing excellent work in the part given to him or her. The work of the artist is at once transcendent work, leading us to God, and deeply humble, rooted in the physical and objective realities that we have.

MOONEY: Thank you for bringing up Maritain. *Art and Scholasticism* is worth reading. Dana Gioia also encouraged me to read Maritain's *Creative Intuition in Art and Poetry,* a series of lectures that he gave at the National Gallery of Art in the 1950s. Maritain passionately argues for the important role of beauty and art as part of the human good and truth-seeking. He explains that much modern thinking has relegated the subconscious to only a place of emotions, drives, and passions that have no intrinsic ordering. Maritain argues that we do have what can be thought of as a Freudian subconscious, but we also have what he calls a spiritual preconscious—a place deep inside of us in our soul where the emotions and reason come together, and we perceive the unity of all things. Maritain describes something along the lines of the experiences that you mentioned, where we encounter a beautiful piece of music, a beautiful work of art, a hike in the mountain that awakens and nurtures that part in our spiritual preconscious where all of reality is integrated. Nurturing that human capacity in the spiritual preconscious allows us to order the passions towards their proper end.

But if we only think of our subconscious in Freudian terms, we don't have a guide for our emotions or passions. Making art and experiencing beauty then become reduced to expression for the sake of expression, not for the sake of truth-seeking. In some strange way, this attempt at self-expression through art actually encloses the self inside itself, cut off from the transcendent we also desire. The view Maritain espouses is that we have a spiritual preconscious, so making art is a reflection of our divine capacity for co-creation in the world. Art for Maritain is more than the self expressing itself; art is a means for understanding the objective world and encountering God.

HARNE: Right. The idea that arts and beauty were bound up with something much greater made much more sense to a society where the arts were also bound up to some form of religious expression and worship. The move toward understanding art and music as a form of self-expression or accessing the deeper, perhaps darker recesses of the soul corresponds historically with a time in which the West is undergoing a profound loss of purpose and its understanding of transcendence.

But it can also work the other way—the spiritual experience in the religious sense can be reawakened as part of a deeper interior life, and the spiritual can be reanimated by the experience and power of beauty.

I've encountered this in liturgical settings, where the beautiful music and what as an Anglican I called the "smells and bells" are present. The reason and will are integrated into a higher synthesis in which truth, goodness, and beauty form a fundamental unity. It doesn't happen often, but it can happen. For me, it happened as a child at a performance of the local symphony performing the first movement of Beethoven's Fifth Symphony. Beauty opened a whole new dimension of the interior life that would never be physically visible yet was no less real. It was dormant but musical beauty first showed me that there was a door and then unlocked it. And then grace can do its work in its own good time.

The deeper spiritual recesses, the non-Freudian preconscious can become a source of spiritual creation in an artistic sense, but those spiritual recesses also have a religious sensibility that can inform and reanimate the soul. Those things have become largely lost in education and culture, but people are still attracted to them, and when we propose ways to recover them, it can be very appealing and dramatic.

MOONEY: I agree. As I've written, Maritain's point is precisely that what he calls poetic knowledge has been lost in modernity. Our modern systems of education focus on scientific knowledge, which is of course important, and also conceptual knowledge, describing the world. But poetic knowledge helps link our experiences in the world, whether in nature or liturgy, back to the spiritual preconscious, and that shapes our work, our everyday lives. Maritain is clear that poetic knowledge is part of the *practical* intellect and therefore is distinct from a mystical experience of God. Poetic knowledge is about our capacity to enter into a contemplative outlook of the world and to engage in contemplative acts of creation. The cost of not philosophically understanding who we are as human beings, or not understanding the integrated part of education, is that we have lost poetic knowledge.

In *Creative Intuition in Art and Poetry,* Maritain discusses specific artistic movements that he thinks are misleading. In particular, he is critical of Surrealism. He goes into the philosophy of the person and asserts that we have the capacity for beauty, but we also have an intellect. He argues that when we understand beauty as passing through the practical intellect and reason, we need to integrate beauty with our reason and practical ways of living. Devoid of this integration into other aspects of our humanity, works of art can be absolutely misleading.

Speaking of the practical intellect, how would you answer concerns that a liberal arts education isn't practical, or that it doesn't prepare students for jobs after graduation?

HARNE: The capacity to speak and think well and to articulate both problems and solutions are skills that are of immediate value in almost any context. This orderly thought, at once, takes in the whole, but can also look at the parts and organize them. Some people who haven't received this education become paralyzed by the complexity of a given situation, but liberal arts graduates have the habits of the mind that are needed to figure out a path forward. These skills are highly valued. There may be a level of technical skill required, depending on the discipline or field, but the formation that liberal arts graduates receive carries them very far.

A friend of mine who received a Great Books education at another institution said that he majored in problem-solving. The problem he faced each time he opened a book was: What does this author mean, how does he or she mean it, and how does this meaning relate to all the books I've read before and fit within the great conversation across time and space? There is a successful marketing company in Chicago that I worked with recently. Its founder is a graduate of a Great Books program, and he says that he uses his education every day. One of Magdalen's trustees says that seventy percent of positions can be learned through training on the job if one has a liberal education. The other thirty percent requires specialized training. But even there, liberal learning is going to be helpful.

When we look at Magdalen's graduates and what they have done, many go on and do graduate work and become teachers or professors, but just as many pursue careers in business or the applied sciences. There is nothing that is ultimately closed to them. We often hear from alumni of Magdalen that even if they had to acquire some specialized training before entering a field like computer science or medicine, that their promotions and later successes came because of their experience with liberal learning. They could solve problems because they had more fully developed their human capacities; they could look at things from a variety of perspectives. Beauty helps in that too. Our success in life is largely dependent on our ability to be fully human in all situations, and the arts and beauty help us accomplish that. They animate parts of us that otherwise remain dormant.

MOONEY: Much of education today promotes a very narrow understanding of problem-solving. There is even a book in the Princeton Public Library with the title *Toilet Trained for Yale*. It is a joke, but it points to how childhood development has been reduced to asking how we produce kids who are going to achieve the right SAT and AP scores to gain admission into highly competitive universities. It is as if all forms of human knowledge are reducible to test scores. Sometimes people even talk about how kindergarten should make five-year-olds college-ready, as if children's instinct for play and music is somehow unrelated to their learning.

I think it's the opposite. Of course, as a child grows, his or her capacity for reasoning and logic grows, too. But we do not want to stamp out of anyone at any age the intuitive attraction to beauty, play and music. We should appreciate these capacities and integrate them with other forms of knowledge, not squash them.

I have seen students who finish their formal college education, and when reflecting on it, they describe themselves as burned out. What was burned out was their creativity and their passion. High-achieving students often equate the good life with climbing the next rung of achievement. I am passionate about bringing beauty and art back into education because I want to fight the burnout culture that affects students, teachers, and professors.

In many places of higher education where I have worked, the fun parts are not fun anymore because they have become competitive. In the workplace and in education, we should be able to integrate beauty, learning, and fun.

How would you respond to the argument that a liberal arts education that integrates beauty is only for the elite who have time for this kind of leisure? Some would say other people need to learn skills, and they need to come out of college with a credential that will prepare them for a job. Is this vision of liberal education, including in art and music, elitist?

HARNE: One of the ways to think this through is to ask again: What is this fundamental anthropology that we all share? If the desire to know is fundamentally human, then education is fundamentally human, and there is something deeply democratic about it. You are providing people with the opportunity to learn and to come to a larger understanding of reality and themselves. Everyone, not just members of an elite, deserve access. In that same fundamental human nature, there is also a desire for beauty, and it transcends many of the class and social barriers that we often think of when we think of what makes something elitist and what does not. The desire to know and to experience the arts of the beautiful is not limited to a particular class.

MOONEY: One of the most transformative classes I ever had was History of Art and Architecture with Vincent Scully. He was a professor at Yale for about sixty years, where he taught generations of students. I will never forget his description of urban redevelopment of cities such as New Haven. He described how highways cut through historic immigrant neighborhoods and how middle-class and lower-income people were geographically and physically cut off from natural beauty. So many low-income public housing projects have no green spaces. If we say that the need for beauty is elitist, and that people who are low-income just need a roof over their heads and food in their mouths, we might dehumanize them in how we build the urban environment. We should not make parks, art, and sculpture accessible only to people who have money.

Unfortunately, the stereotype that the need for beauty is elitist remains common. For people who have an instinctive dislike for anything perceived as elitist, how do you move past that in talking about art? How do you avoid turning people off to the topic of beauty?

HARNE: That is a challenge, and it's part of the work of a good teacher. If a teacher is convinced that there is amazing food in a room that has an incredible taste and that is also incredibly good for the student, she will try to find a doorway in to get the student there. It may require all sorts of things to reach this goal; it may require juggling, storytelling, or enormous amounts of creativity. These are the gifts of the teacher. If I am trying to introduce my students to something that I think will nurture their souls and humanize them, I will start where they are and find a pathway.

There are many challenges when you want to popularize the study of beauty, and the purist might not want to deal with them, but the teacher will find a way to open the doors to beauty. My children are fans of the *Magic Tree House* series by Mary Pope Osborne. She does an excellent job of introducing figures such as Leonardo da Vinci and Louis Armstrong into her books, laying the groundwork for further exploration. This past summer, we saw an adaptation of one of her books for the stage for children. I sat in that auditorium watching kids, many of them from public schools, learning about Shakespeare, experiencing an introduction to the Bard in a way that was completely accessible. The children were on the edge of their seats; they loved it and lived in that moment. That is how it ought to be.

If someone is older and perhaps resistant, I would say to find the cultural or ethnic tradition that they most strongly identify with and look for the fine arts within it. Begin there and introduce themselves to their forebears in the artistic world; that is a place to start.

MOONEY: Dana Gioia, who grew up in a blue-collar environment with Mexican and Italian immigrant parents, has a lot to say about why beauty matters for people who will be going into blue-collar professions. In societies that I have studied, like Haiti, many of the people there are natural poets and compose and perform music. There are plenty of resources about beauty to draw on that are not elitist, and there is no shortage of art museums or musical performances that make experiences of beauty affordable and open to people of all income levels.

How would you suggest that teachers interact with students who don't immediately show an affinity with beauty in art and music or who have been trained by society to be suspicious of beauty?

HARNE: In the town where Magdalen is, there was for a long time an old, beat-up truck parked on the street, rusted and falling apart. There was a bumper sticker on the back of it that I was quite fond of, which said, "Nature always bats last." For me, it inspired hope that no matter what we do culturally, the nature of things will eventually reassert itself.

There is something deeply democratic about both the fine arts and the liberal arts. If Aristotle is right that all men by nature desire to know, then we are all wired for the liberal arts. Is it true that, analogously, all people desire beauty? If so, then both knowing and delighting in beauty are at the root of a common humanity and inform a fundamental solidarity across all other social divisions.

I never give up on a student regardless of his or her age or background. I introduce beautiful objects and the conditions for contemplation and silence. Often, after initial reluctance, this resistance can be overcome through friendship, encouragement, and patience. We do not have infinite time and patience for every single student, but it is possible to make these things available.

I do not have exactly the same background as Dana Gioia, but I am a first-generation college student myself. I remember my first trip to a local symphony to hear Beethoven. I suppose that if anybody had asked, "Do you think George is going to respond favorably to this?" that they would have said, "No, forget about it. He can't sit still. We can't do anything with him." But they put me on a bus and took me to the symphony, and that changed my life forever.

DISCUSSION QUESTIONS

1. Harne reflects, "How much wiser would our citizens be if they came to understand the parts and wholes of our society, the places where things

can be resolved and where they cannot, and the fundamental practice of thinking in terms of purpose (*telos*)!" Particularly telling in this reflection is the acknowledgement that some tensions in society are simply unresolvable. Do you agree? If so, what are these unfixable parts? How does society go about giving voice to these parts of its brokenness? How can it go about tolerating them in a way that promotes healthy functioning of the whole?

2. Discuss: "Experiences of beauty need not stop in the moment something grabs our attention." For example, can you recall a time you experienced something beautiful and the memory has stayed with you? Would you say what Maritain calls the spiritual preconscious was awakened by that experience?

3. What do you make of Harne's notion that art ought to be more of a work of transcendence, rather than of self-expression? Do you agree? Does one need to have a concept of the divine in order to embrace this notion of transcendence?

4. What forms of art and beauty have you engaged in, or are currently engaged in, that animate parts of yourself that would have otherwise "lie dormant"? Furthermore, Harne references alumni of Magdalen College who report that in their introduction to certain works of art and beauty in college, "They could solve problems because they were more fully human; they could look at things from a variety of perspectives. Beauty helps in that too. Our success in life is largely dependent on our ability to be fully human in all situations." Have your experiences of beauty had similar effects on you?

5. Harne describes how he fell in love with music when he attended a symphony. Was music a part of your early life and education? Did you ever have an experience that made you fall in love with music?

6. One meaning of the liberal arts Harne and Mooney discuss are the classical trivium (grammar, logic, and rhetoric) and quadrivium (arithmetic, astronomy, music, and geometry). Do you agree that these fields all constitute the primary forms of knowing? If you have not formally studied all of them in school, are there ways to continue learning about these fields?

7. Does the notion that beauty is related to order and truth make sense to you? Or confound you? Why?

8. Harne disagrees with the common objections that beauty mis-leads us from the truth, or that beauty is elitist. Do you agree or disagree with him? Why?

REFERENCES

Aristotle. *The Nicomachean Ethics.* Translated by David Ross. Oxford: Oxford University Press, 2009.

Benjamin, Walter. "The Work of Art in the Age of Mechanical Reproducibility." In *Walter Benjamin: Selected Writings, Volume 3 (1935–1938).* Cambridge: The Belknap Press of Harvard University Press, 2002.

Boethius. *Boethian Number Theory: A Translation of the "De Institutione Arithmetica."* Translated by Michael Masi. Amsterdam: Rodopi, 1983.

______. *Fundamentals of Music*. Edited by Calvin Bower. New Haven: Yale University Press, 1989.

Gilson, Étienne. *Arts of the Beautiful*. Normal: Dalkey Archive Press, 2000.

______. *Forms and Substances in the Arts*. Translated by Salvator Atlanasio. Normal: Dalkey Archive Press, 2001.

Gioia, Dana. "Why Beauty Matters." *First Things*, February 18, 2020, at www.firstthings.com/media/why-beauty-matters.

Leclercq, Jean. *The Love of Learning and The Desire for God: A Study of Monastic Culture*. 3rd edition. New York: Fordham University Press, 1982.

Maritain, Jacques. *Art and Scholasticism*. Providence: Cluny Media, 2016.

Maritain, Jacques. *Creative Intuition in Art and Poetry*. Introduction by Raymond Hain. Providence: Cluny Media, 2019.

Mooney, Margarita A. "Engineering, Beauty and a Longing for the Infinite." *Scientific American Blog Network*, October 22, 2019, at blogs.scientificamerican.com/observations/engineering-beauty-and-a-longing-for-the-infinite/.

Newman, John Henry. *The Idea of a University Defined and Illustrated: In Nine Discourses Delivered to the Catholics of Dublin*. Chicago: Loyola University Press, 1927.

Osborne, Mary Pope. *Magic Tree House Books*. New York: Random House Children's Books, 2008.

Pieper, Josef. *Leisure: The Basis of Culture*. San Francisco: Ignatius Press, 2009.

______. *Only the Lover Sings: Art and Contemplation.* San Francisco: Ignatius Press, 1990.

Scruton, Roger. *Beauty: A Very Short Introduction.* Illustrated edition. Oxford: Oxford University Press, 2011.

ADDITIONAL READINGS

Bernstein, Leonard. *The Unanswered Question: Six Talks at Harvard.* Revised edition. Cambridge: Harvard University Press, 1981.

Blum, Christopher, and Joshua Hochschild. *A Mind at Peace: Reclaiming an Ordered Soul in the Age of Distraction.* Manchester: Sophia Institute Press, 2017.

Copland, Aaron. *What to Listen for in Music.* Illustrated edition. New York: Signet, 2011.

Dewey, John. *Art as Experience.* New York: TarcherPerigee, 2005.

Gombrich, E. H. *The Story of Art.* London: Phaidon Press, 1995.

Plato. *Plato's Symposium.* Translated by Seth Benardete. Chicago: University of Chicago Press, 2001.

______. *The Republic of Plato.* Translated by Allan Bloom. New York: Basic Books, 1968.

Shrimpton, Paul. *The "Making of Men": The Idea and Reality of Newman's University in Oxford and Dublin.* London: Gracewing Publishing, 2014.

Stravinsky, Igor. *Poetics of Music in the Form of Six Lessons.* Revised edition. Cambridge: Harvard University Press, 1970.

ROOSEVELT MONTÁS was born in the Dominican Republic and moved to New York City as a teenager, where he attended public schools in Queens. He went on to Columbia College, Columbia University, where he studied comparative literature and philosophy. In 2003, he completed a Ph.D. in English, also at Columbia, and began teaching in the faculty of the English Department in 2004. In 2008, he was appointed Director of the Center for the Core Curriculum, a position he held for 10 years. Currently, he is Senior Lecturer in American Studies and English at Columbia. Roosevelt specializes in Antebellum American literature and culture, with a particular interest in American national identity. His dissertation, *Rethinking America: Abolitionism and the Antebellum Transformation of the Discourse of National Identity*, won Columbia University's 2004 Bancroft Award. In 2000, he received the Presidential Award for Outstanding Teaching by a Graduate Student. He teaches moral and political philosophy in the Columbia Core Curriculum as well as seminars in American literature and culture in the American Studies Program. Each summer, he teaches a course in political theory and citizenship to high school students from low-income families through Columbia's *Freedom and Citizenship* program. He speaks and writes on the history, meaning, and future of liberal education, and is writing a book entitled *Rescuing Socrates: How the Great Books Changed My Life and Why They Matter for a New Generation* (Princeton University Press (2021).

CHAPTER 7

Is a Liberal Arts Education Elitist?

ROOSEVELT MONTÁS *and* MARGARITA A. MOONEY

MOONEY: There's a common criticism that I get when I talk about liberal arts education—that it's elitist, only for the privileged. You and I have a unique perspective on this question, thanks to our shared cultural and educational backgrounds. We are both Hispanic, and we have Ivy League pedigrees. In some ways, we have both felt very privileged in our education. But we also have a passion to share what we have learned with a broader public.

Let's begin with your personal biography. How did you come to the United States, and how did you come to fall in love with liberal arts education?

MONTÁS: I am from the Dominican Republic. I came to the United States at the age of twelve, not speaking English, with my older brother and our single mother. I went to the zoned public schools in New York City—the middle school and high school that were in my neighborhood. By extraordinarily good fortune, I ended up at Columbia University as an undergraduate, where I encountered its Core Curriculum.

This required set of courses is sometimes called a Great Books program because there is such an emphasis on classical texts, but students also study art and music. This course of study changed the way I look at the world. It gave me a sense of the importance and power of a liberal arts education as well as a sense of personal mission.

The central, organizing principle in my intellectual endeavors and academic career has been to deepen and promote an understanding of liberal arts education—just as the Scala Foundation's mission puts it—for all. That is, I want to break down the barriers of exclusivity that have sometimes been thrown up around liberal arts education as a way of precisely reinforcing class and privilege. I want to show that a liberal arts education is meant to *liberate,* to free, to empower.

I want to break down the barriers of exclusivity that have sometimes been thrown up around liberal arts education as a way of precisely reinforcing class and privilege. I want to show that a liberal arts education is meant to liberate, *to free, to empower.*

MOONEY: What does a liberal education via the Core Curriculum at Columbia look like?

MONTÁS: The Core Curriculum begins with a year-long course in literature that every first-year student takes. They start with Homer's *Iliad* and then proceed to other classical texts loosely in the Western tradition of literary expression: the Greek playwrights and historians, the Hebrew Bible, the New Testament, etc. It proceeds all the way up to the present, so that at the very end of the year we end up reading contemporary novels. As of 2020, Toni Morrison's *Song of Solomon* capped the curriculum.

Sophomores take another year-long course in philosophical texts that grapples with fundamental questions. It begins with Plato, followed by Aristotle, and other ancient writers, through Augustine, Aquinas, Cicero, and then it proceeds into the Renaissance and the Enlightenment. Finally, it comes all the way to the present. The art and music courses follow a similar path.

Behind the curriculum is the notion that exposing students to some of the most significant and provocative texts from the past, texts that have proven to be particularly illuminating of fundamental human experiences, is a powerful way of conducting a liberal education. Students encounter texts that deal with great questions, with persistent, enduring existential questions of the human condition, and they encounter and debate those texts.

At Columbia we emphasize the commonality of intellectual experience. The whole first-year class reads the same books at the same time for the entire year. All twelve hundred students, in the middle of October, are reading the *Oresteia*; then in the first week of December, they're reading the gospel of Luke. In April, they're all reading Dostoyevsky's *Crime and Punishment*. And they do the same thing as sophomores—they follow a common schedule of readings for the entire year. That has a very powerful impact in creating community, facilitating dialogue, and linking students to a broader, larger intellectual landscape.

Within this common experience, students and professors meet in small classes to discuss great texts. The student learns by an organic process of dialogue with the teacher and others. You cannot have a liberal education program with very large classes. Liberal learning has to be interactive. You have to be able to guide the groups of students in such a way that there is exchange. A liberal education can only be delivered in a kind of artisanal way. You cannot mass-produce it.

This is all in contrast to much of higher education today, which is dominated by disciplines, with liberal education poorly taught as introductions to one or another disciplinary study. For example, many literature classes really only teach how to be a graduate student in literature, forgoing how to relate their own discipline to other disciplines or fundamental human questions. Columbia's Core Curriculum benefits the faculty as well, by forcing them to move away from their own disciplinary specialties and teach within this common non-disciplinary educational project.

MOONEY: Why do some people charge that the content of the Core Curriculum is elitist and that it reproduces privilege and excludes minority voices?

MONTÁS: These courses in Columbia's Core Curriculum have been in place for about a hundred years. They were developed during a period in history when higher education was indeed only for the privileged. In the late nineteenth and early twentieth centuries, higher education in the United States meant, essentially, liberal education. Because liberal education was available only to the few, there is a historical association between liberal education and privilege.

But the story of American education, until recently, has been the story of an ever-widening field of access to higher education for more and more people. That has also meant a wider field of access to liberal education, which is how you and I were able to get a liberal education, and why today we need to continue to fight for the accessibility of liberal education for all.

There are people who believe that a traditional liberal arts curriculum is not appropriate for the kind of diversity that we have in our student body today. In higher education, we now have more minorities, more immigrants, more people from low socioeconomic backgrounds, more first-generation students, and more women. The critique is that this curriculum is no longer appropriate for that population.

I am sympathetic to those critiques and I can see how intuitive that notion is, but there is a profound danger in it. It is condescending to this diverse student population to suppose that these great texts, which have been so influential in shaping our contemporary world, can't speak to them, that they are somehow inaccessible and that the human experience they explore is irrelevant to our diverse student body. That is a fundamental misconception.

I'll give you two examples. The first is my own: When I read authors like Plato and Saint Augustine and Montaigne, they connected with some of the deepest parts of me. I saw myself reflected in those writers, not because they were Dominican, not because they shared my cultural heritage, but because they shared something of my own human experience and they illuminated it in a particular way.

A second example is a student I had a couple of years ago. Every summer I teach in a program for rising high school seniors, all of them low-income students who will be the first ones to go to college in their families. I had a student from Harlem who had grown up in foster homes, whose mother had a drug addiction problem. This really extraordinary young woman showed up in the classroom and we read Plato's *Apology* and the *Crito*. She found herself affirmed and spoken to by the figure of Socrates, and she ended up going to a liberal arts college. She graduated a year ago with a major in philosophy. When they conferred prizes on her at graduation, her professors explicitly compared her to Socrates.

Those are just examples of the way in which the power that these ideas, figures, and texts have is not circumscribed by class or culture.

These texts are important precisely because they transcend the limitations of class and culture from which they come.

MOONEY: So in some ways liberal arts education *is* elitist, if by elitist we mean that there is a standard of excellence. The works on the Core Curriculum are excellent precisely because they transcend boundaries. They might be rooted in a particular historical experience, but you're saying that a work can both be grounded in a particular experience and can transcend it. It's when those two qualities are present that a work becomes excellent, not in an exclusionary sense of elitism, but in the sense of an elite standard that recognizes that certain works blend particularly and universality better than others.

MONTÁS: Yes! Another example of that is Toni Morrison, who now caps the literature course in the Core Curriculum. Morrison is rooted in a particular history—a history as a black woman in America, a descendant of slaves. What makes her an extraordinary author is not just the particularity of her experience, but her capacity to convey that particularity in a way that somebody who does not share her experience is able to grasp its humanity. Somebody who does not have a slave ancestor, who is not American, who is not a woman, and who is not black can read Toni Morrison and still understand the human experience that she is describing. She is able to describe a particular case in terms that are universally accessible. *That* is excellence.

Now, there is a system of critique that says that there is no such thing as excellence, that all value judgments are in fact ways of coding certain forms of power and privilege. We need to take this critique seriously because, indeed, there have historically been forms of exclusion that are built around ideas of excellence.

But we can have insights and heighten our critical awareness of the ways in which the discourse of excellence has been used to reinforce certain power structures, all without giving up the notion of human excellence. In fact, we should *not* give up the notion of human excellence, since to critique one form of power is to invoke a higher ideal and, from that basis, to critique an unjust distribution of power. We cannot make any such judgment unless we hold some idea of excellence, some idea of the good. And a liberal education is precisely a kind of education that concerns itself with investigating the very notions of human good and human excellence.

MOONEY: When people hear of the Core Curriculum, they often assume it's never adapted. But in fact, Toni Morrison being on the Core Curriculum is an example of an excellent and relatively recent work of literature. To put her work on the same syllabus as great books from thousands of years of history is to show students that newer works can match up to these criteria of excellence. A liberal arts education can help them see that their experience, regardless of what it is, can also rise to this same level of excellence.

MONTÁS: Truly, there is no ultimate or final list of essential works. We are always tinkering, always discovering new things. When we choose a set of works to organize a liberal education around, it is always provisional. As Columbia does, we should always be rethinking which books are most effective in conveying and promoting human flourishing.

Let me give an historical example: coming out of the American Civil War and the abolition of slavery in the late nineteenth century, there was a foundational debate between the two most prominent leaders in the African American community, W. E. B. Du Bois, a classically trained intellectual, and Booker T. Washington, a figure who was born into slavery and overcame great adversity to lead a movement for economic advancement.

Washington thought that upon coming out of slavery the free African American population ought to focus on practical education and economic self-sufficiency, even if that meant accepting a second-class citizenship.

Du Bois was entirely against that notion. He said that we need the highest kinds of education—not just practical education, but also liberal education for African American youth. He said famously, "I sit with Shakespeare and he winces not." That is, Du Bois found that Shakespeare was as much his own as he was his white classmates at Harvard and his white German colleagues while studying abroad. The classical learning tradition, he insisted, the *liberatory* tradition, properly belongs to everyone. Du Bois called on the universality of the liberal tradition to empower the project of civil rights and equal citizenship.

MOONEY: I relate to this point personally. I'll never forget walking through Phelps Gate at Yale and being overwhelmed at the beauty of symbols of that institution's traditions. In some ways, I did not feel entirely like I fit in. I didn't have an elite prep school education. I didn't think I could compete with my peers academically. Yet we shared an excitement about inquiry and learning.

I relished the fact that I made my first Jewish friend, who became my roommate and one of my closest friends. I met people from the upper class, who had wealth that was beyond anything I had imagined. I met people from middle-class backgrounds, and I also met people from Hispanic backgrounds and many African Americans. Yet, the educational experience I shared with my fellow students was something that bonded us together—not annihilating our differences, but rather working through them to a kind of unity around the love of learning.

What is it about this shared love of learning that is actually capable of creating a sense of unity among students?

MONTÁS: We might ask, "What makes a work of fiction, philosophy, or art a *classic*?" Many have grappled with this question, but a useful description is that a classic is a work that people continue to find meaningful a long time after it was written or created. That is, there are some works that, generation after generation, have proved their capacity to illuminate across humanity, to enrich and give depth to our lives. Through these works we learn the meaning of our own humanity. They encourage us and equip us to become more fully ourselves.

These texts also have a certain complexity that makes them irreducible to ideological manipulation. They are multifaceted.

That's why the study of the classics is important to realize the promise of diversity. At Columbia, we have a fairly diverse student body. The liberal arts classroom provides an enriching environment to discuss our human commonality in conjunction with the different nodes of humanity.

MOONEY: When talking about whether liberal arts education is just for the privileged, it's important not to just simply assume that one's place of privilege or disadvantage is deterministic of one's moral conscience. In my experience at Yale, across many social boundaries, the classics shaped our very notion of ourselves—not in a way that eradicated our individuality, but rather in a way that expanded our identities in order to be better able to find modes of connecting to other people who may come from very different backgrounds.

And outside of higher education, I have seen the same thing in the people I have met and worked with in Haiti and Central America, as well as in my own family. In every human person there is a conscience that has freedom and can transcend one's social location. A free human conscience is not a capacity unique to the elite, or to member of any particular social group. It's universal.

MONTÁS: A liberal education is premised on the notion of human freedom. It is the kind of education that is appropriate to a free individual, a free subject, which means that it presumes the capacity for self-transcendence—the capacity in the student to overcome the determinations of birth, class, gender, and society. It is because we are capable of activating our own freedom and rising above ourselves that we are subjects of liberal education.

I find the life story of Frederick Douglass to be one of the most inspiring and illustrative examples of the meaning of education for freedom. Here's a passage from his first autobiography, *Narrative of the Life of an American Slave*:

> Very soon after I went to live with Mr. and Mrs. Auld, she very kindly commenced to teach me the A, B, C. After I had learned this, she assisted me in learning to spell words of three or four letters. Just at this point of my progress, Mr. Auld found out what was going on, and at once forbade Mrs. Auld to instruct me further, telling her, among other things, that it was unlawful, as well as unsafe, to teach a slave to read...I now understood what had been to me a most perplexing difficulty—to wit, the white man's power to enslave the black man. From that moment, I understood the pathway from slavery to freedom.

Douglass discovered a pathway from slavery to freedom. He sees how the world would be opened up to him via literacy and education when his master tries to stop him. Read his biography—it's an extraordinary journey. That liberating notion animates our understanding of true education.

Today, although there is no longer chattel slavery in the U.S., there are other forms of slavery all around us, forms of subjugation, coercion, and domination. One of the most pervasive is what has been called wage slavery. That's when you sell your labor for a period of time and are, during that time, completely subject to someone else's authority.

This form of slavery was recognized even in antiquity. In his famous book *On Duties,* Marcus Tullius Cicero says that whoever gives his labor for money sells himself and puts himself in the rank of slaves. It's almost taken for granted today that this is okay, that it's some kind of way of life to sell yourself to servitude and dehumanization from Monday to Friday in order to buy the privilege of relaxing on the weekends. But it's not so. That is not the worthiest life for a human being. There is little dignity in that; on the contrary, it's a degrading brutalization of human freedom. So, it's not right that education should just be about preparing students to sell some portion of their humanity for wages.

It's not right that education should just be about preparing students to sell some portion of their humanity for wages.

Yes, of course education should give you skills and competencies that should help you make a living, but there is also a higher calling for education. Education should also be about how to be free, about how to live the life of a free individual, not just the life of a hired laborer. As W. E. B. Du Bois would put it in his essay "Of the Wings of Atalanta," in the book *Souls of Black Folk* (1903): "The true college will ever have but one goal: not to earn meat but to know the end and aim of the life which meat nourishes."

In his work *On Duties*, Cicero said, "The search for truth and its investigation are, above all, peculiar to man. Therefore, when we are free from necessary business and other concerns, we are eager to see and to hear or to learn considering that the discovery of obscure and wonderful things is necessary for a blessed life."

I love that idea, that the discovery of obscure or wonderful things is necessary for a blessed life.

Did you know that the Greek word *scholé*, from which we get the word school, means leisure? School is not supposed to be about work but about what you do when you don't have to work. And what do you do when you don't have to work? You delight in the discovery of obscure or wonderful things. Thank you, Cicero.

MOONEY: Thank you, Cicero! The idea that the search for truth leads to a blessed life resonates with what Jacques Maritain says: to educate the human conscience is both the means and the ends of education. Education shapes the whole person, and it has to begin with working on one's conscience that is created for freedom.

Some might say that this kind of education sounds idealistic—it's just not realistic to educate in this manner in public schools, or even in many private schools. Is it possible to educate this way in the kinds of educational settings we currently have?

MONTÁS: I have to say, yes, it is possible. Otherwise, we should all just quit and go home right now and have a couple of drinks and numb ourselves.

Although I myself am a product of the New York City schools, the phrase I use to describe these large urban systems of public education is "failure by design." If you saw those schools listed in a catalogue, you would say, "Yeah, that's going to fail most people. As a system, that is not going to be successful."

But many teachers work against the system. Many teachers succeed in changing lives, in countering the noxious effects of the institutional structures. I would not have made it to where I have without some teachers that did what Plato said about reorienting you and making you look in the right direction. So, it *is* possible. It is possible not because of the system but despite that system.

MOONEY: A lot of people feel that they don't have a lot of power to influence larger structures, and they're not exactly wrong. But at the same time, if a movement came along to change those structures, you would need the people in place to carry out that vision. The model of education we are talking about is a calling. I don't want people in a structure that doesn't support their vision of education to feel frustrated and leave. Believe me, I've often wondered why I can't do more to affect large institutions.

It's also important to note that educational problems aren't just confined to poor urban public schools. To put it bluntly, there are plenty of dysfunctional students coming out of suburban, elite schools. They may not have low socio-economic resources, but the problems of loss of personal identity, nihilism, drug abuse, and mental illness are ravaging wealthy schools. Those students' parents may be professionals, and they may live in attractive zip codes, but education isn't serving them very well either. We should care about educating all students well, regardless of whether or not they have socioeconomic privilege.

Even if one person can't change the overall conditions in a school, any teacher can have an impact on individual students, beginning with caring about them personally.

MONTÁS: Exactly. The first thing that matters is whether teachers care about students. That's step one. If the students do not get a sense that you care about them as individuals, it's game over. It is only through that bond of trust, affection, and human connection that education happens.

You can get a lot of instruction from watching videos without any relationship at all, but I don't consider that education. Education is cultivation into a particular community, and that requires interaction. Obviously, there are technologically mediated forms of interaction, and those count towards building community. But whatever the medium, the bond of a human being connecting with another human being is a pre-condition for education to happen.

MOONEY: One of my students in the Scala seminar commented that our intensive summer program felt like being in a big family (she should know, since she's from a family of eight)—where you have long open-ended debates with lots of different perspectives. You don't all get along, you don't all agree, and you don't always like each other, but you somehow stick together.

Friendship in an educational setting is a commitment to a journey together. It's not the same as having someone to go out with on the weekend just for entertainment or pleasure. For liberal education to happen, there needs to be a shared commitment to the journey grounded in true friendship. James B. Murphy wrote in his article, "Why a Core?" that a core curriculum helps unite students around a shared intellectual journey, as they are reading the same books during the same semesters. Because so few schools have a core curriculum, a lot of students are missing that kind of commitment and deep friendships around learning.

It can also be extremely difficult for teachers to know the character of their students when they only see them in the classroom for a few hours a week. Since there are not many opportunities to informally interact with students and learn their personal stories, I host dinners at my house, or try to show up at events on campus, or go with students to places where the conversations just naturally arise like the dining hall.

Some educators are actually afraid of having personal relationships with students outside of class. Some of that comes from a fear of being accused of inappropriate behavior. Others fear a loss of authority. But there are ways to set appropriate boundaries and create the right dynamics. We can get to know our students as people, and still retain a sense of authority.

In fact, we shouldn't forget that students look to their teachers as role models. Many students are actually looking for a moral authority who's not their parent. When they don't encounter anybody in their education who they can look up to, they don't connect what they're learning in the classroom to a person who knows how to live a coherent life and can guide them in using their freedom, making moral commitments, and developing life projects. It's important to create educational settings where the authority of educators is part of a shared journey towards a beautiful life.

Montás: An effective teacher uses his or her authority to help the students onward toward their own understanding. I often turn to this quote from Plato's *Republic*:

> Education isn't what some people declare it to be, namely, putting knowledge into souls that lack it, like putting sight

> into blind eyes. But our present discussion, on the other hand, shows that the power to learn is present in everyone's soul and that the instrument with which each learns is like an eye that cannot be turned from darkness to light without turning the whole body. Then education is the craft concerned with doing this very thing, this turning around, and with how the soul can most easily and effectively be made to do it. It isn't the craft of putting sight into the soul. Education takes for granted that sight is there but that it isn't turned the right way or looking where it ought to look and tries to redirect it appropriately.

This analogy of eyesight is illuminating. When the eye is open, it cannot help but see. When the mind encounters a truth, it can't resist accepting it. That's why Plato speaks here about a turning around, a redirection of capacities that are inherent in the human soul.

Something of this insight is captured in the very word "education." Education comes from the Latin verb *educere,* which means "to lead out." True education concerns the tapping of innate capacities that each of us carry inside of us. Plato's teacher Socrates had a famous doctrine that all knowledge is recollection. When we learn something, Socrates argued, we are only becoming aware of what we already knew. All a teacher can do is turn your intellectual eyesight in the right direction. Ralph Waldo Emerson put the same insight this way in his "Divinity School Address": "Truly speaking, it is not instruction but provocation that I can receive from another soul." I always say that education happens by contagion, not by transmission. It's something that you catch.

Mooney: With regards to answers to life's great questions, there is substantial disagreement over what those are, or whether even truth exists.

Many college faculty today are skeptical of anyone proposing a conception of the human person grounded in moral certainty. Does this make liberal education an incoherent project—asking questions to which there are no right or wrong answers?

MONTÁS: Yes, there is a collapse of consensus among college faculty on what students should learn, and whether anything is ultimately true. However, a true liberal education does not impose one view of human nature or of the human good. What it advances is a shared commitment to its investigation. It is precisely because the nature of the human good is inherently contestable that we engage liberal learning, a kind of learning that involves inner transformation rather than absorption of some pre-established truth. The problem comes from the too-facile assumption that the teacher knows the answer, and that we're just going to lead students to it.

The ultimate subject of inquiry in liberal education is the human good. It is precisely engaging in that inquiry that constitutes liberal education—not *answering* but *asking* what is the ultimate human good. It is a red herring to say that we shouldn't do it because we can't agree on what the answer is.

MOONEY: There's also a difference between saying that the questions are important and debatable, but there are good answers, and saying that we should remain skeptical that the question is ultimately unanswerable at all.

MONTÁS: Which is, ultimately, nihilism.

MOONEY: Right. And some faculty are in each of the two camps.

MONTÁS: Some faculty are nihilists.

MOONEY: Even for those who aren't, many faculty, especially at secular universities, recoil at the notion that one of the ends of higher education is the formation of a human person towards particular ends. That feels as if they would be using their conception of what that end is to impose their personal viewpoint on the students. Most faculty no longer feel as if their viewpoint comes from a coherent tradition with a vision of what those proper human ends are. Even if you have individual faculty members who might have convictions about the importance of moral formation among students, many are very hesitant to speak about those convictions.

But then how will the students they teach learn to develop their own moral commitments? I recently spoke with a young teacher at a public charter school that is classically inspired, where the teachers are encouraged to read more great texts and have discussions through a staff-wide Socratic seminar. It turns out that the teachers themselves don't have a coherent personal identity as adults, they're still searching, and they don't have the tools to find that inner light for themselves. One of her colleagues said at a seminar, "Whatever your grandma says, you don't really believe that truth anymore. Truth changes every generation." The staff then arrived at an impasse: "Well, if truth changes every generation, what are we supposed to do with our children?" The seminar was supposed to inspire staff to find truth, but because many teachers lacked their own moral commitments, the training actually made them despair a little.

MONTÁS: Stories like that remind us that liberal education is a countercultural practice. That is, we are engaged in offering a challenge to the prevailing cultural ethos in which we live. What you are describing I think is the stream that we swim against, and that's what we're here to do.

What you get in our students, in our faculty, in our peers, both at the higher education level and at the primary and secondary levels, is a reflection of the contemporary ethos of materialist, consumerist, almost nihilist culture in which we live, where we have no confidence to claim to know anything at all. We are operating within and against this post-modern condition. Socrates, who in some ways is the paradigmatic figure in this project of reviving classical liberal arts education, was executed by his fellow citizens. He was condemned to death by his peers for engaging in precisely an activity that challenged the culture.

We're swimming against a very strong stream, but that's just what I want to do. I want to be swimming against the stream. That's my job, why I went into this.

At the center of the project of liberal education is not the subject matter. It's not the skills, or the knowledge, or the information, but the student's development. Unfortunately, increased professionalization is a big source of pressure on liberal education—that is, an emphasis on education being practical in terms of making a career. We see that everywhere. There is a shrinking of funding and availability for liberal arts in favor of an emphasis on technical education, vocational education, and pre-professional education. We live in a free-market society that emphasizes productivity, efficiency, and cash value.

In Book VIII of the *Politics*, Aristotle said, "There is a certain kind of education that children must be given not because it is useful or necessary but because it is noble and suitable for a free person." The name that we have for this is liberal education. The mission of Scala, to promote the liberal arts for all, is quite critical in this moment in social history.

Mooney: How do we help young people form a coherent personal identity that will help guide them through their education, regardless of what field that is? So many students that I work with really lack a sense of belonging or vocation. Frankly, the most heartwarming things students have ever said to me are not just that I've shaped how they think about a particular subject but that they feel like they can come and simply talk with me when they have questions about life that don't really have answers. This requires being able to sit with them in the mystery of life, which is a gift.

For example, I've had long conversations with a student who lost both his mother and his father during graduate school. I accompanied another student as he battled cancer, dying at the age of twenty-six. There's no nice, coherent, tight philosophical or even theological answer to this kind of suffering, but it is possible to open your mind and your heart to face these ultimate questions in a way that integrates our human capacity for knowledge and for love.

This leads me to ask: What may be on many people's minds during a pandemic like COVID-19? What is the value of a liberal education during a crisis?

MONTÁS: As crises often do, this crisis has brought our own humanity into greater focus: our frailty, our mortality (the defining feature of our life), and the centrality of bonds and human connection in our sense of self. The quarantine most of us underwent has made us realize how much we need community and human contact.

Many of us have found solace in returning to some of the classic books. I've been reading Giovanni Boccaccio's *Decameron* because of its focus on the Black Death. This crisis brings into relief the very values and questions that a liberal arts education is concerned with, and those of us who have access to such an education find ourselves with an extra set of tools.

Also, there's a story I think about in the Pali Canon, which is the oldest collection of teachings from the historical Buddha. In "The Smile of the Mountains," the Buddha is talking to one of his disciples, a local king. He says: "What do you think, great king? Suppose a man, trustworthy and reliable, were to come to you from the east and on arrival would say, 'If it please Your Majesty, you should know that I come from the east. There I saw a great mountain as high as the clouds coming this way, crushing all living beings in its path. Do whatever you think should be done.'" This happens again, with men from the west, north, and south. The Buddha continues, "If, great king, such a great peril should arise, such a terrible destruction of human life—the human state being so hard to obtain—what should be done?" The king replies, "If, Lord, such a great peril should arise, such a terrible destruction of human life—the human life being so hard to obtain—what else should be done but Dhamma-conduct, right conduct, skillful deeds, meritorious deeds?"

And I imagine the Buddha took a small pause here. Then he resumes, "I inform you, great king—I announce to you, great king—aging and death are rolling in on you. When aging and death are rolling in on you, great king, what should be done?"

You might think this is very depressing, but let me remind you what Montaigne said: You don't die because you're sick, you die because you're alive. You cannot be truly alive except through a vivid apprehension of your death. The tools of a liberal education help us to face these questions around suffering and death.

Mooney: I recently re-read C. S. Lewis's "Learning in War-Time," an oration he gave at St. Mary of the Virgin in Oxford in 1939 just after England had entered the Second World War. I re-read that essay to help me get through this time of being cut off from my community. Lewis notes that even in wartime, we don't cease being fully human. If we don't feed our minds with good literature and good ideas, he says, we will be deformed. The life of the mind requires fighting distractions, and in a time of crisis, you have to really practice fighting those distractions.

Times of isolation can be a good chance to enjoy solitude with the Great Books, rather than getting sucked into the depressing around-the-clock news cycle. At one point, when I was sick of screen time, I sat down with a pad of paper and *The Divine Comedy*, which I had never read. In that deep solitude with my Great Book and my notebook, it dawned on me: I'm having a great conversation with Dante. This object he created called *The Divine Comedy* is an expression of the man, the actual historical man named Dante. It was like I was doing *lectio divina*—a Benedictine way of reading scripture slowly, meditatively, open to converting one's heart—but with a great work of literature. It dawned on me that this is actually a wonderful way to read great books, and an approach open to anyone at any stage of life or education.

But to anybody who has not had the benefits of a formal Great Books education, I want to offer the encouragement that you *can* pick up the great classics and read them, finding inspiration. You might need a guide (just as Dante needed Virgil), you might need a community, but find out what's being taught in the Great Books, and pick one up and let that enrich your mind and your soul. Invite other people to read and discuss those books. Then, when a crisis comes, you'll find yourself responding to it from a deeper place of understanding of humanity and of your own identity.

MONTÁS: I could not agree more. Let's give some thought not just to what's happened in the last twenty-four hours, but the last twenty-four centuries.

In Book I of the *Politics,* Aristotle says, "A complete community comes to be for the sake of living, but it remains in existence for the sake of living well."

DISCUSSION QUESTIONS

1. Montás says that it is condescending to suppose that someone won't be interested in reading great texts. Have you ever felt condescended to in your education? How did you respond?

2. Montás argues that a Great Books education raises universal questions about the human good that should be debated. What is the role of debate and disagreement around fundamental questions of truth and goodness?

3. Montás notes that liberal learning must be interactive. Do you think our increased reliance on distance-learning in models of higher education offers more benefits or harms for such interaction? In what ways can digital learning truly be interactive so that promotes liberal learning? In which ways can it not?

4. Think of a character in a classical work of literature with whom you closely identify, or who taught you something about yourself. Why is this? Is this particular character similar to you in many respects, or are you actually quite different from one another with regard to gender, socioeconomic status, race, historical location, physical location, etc?

5. Montás identified Toni Morrison as one such contemporary author whose work he teaches in his Great Books curriculum. Which recent

works might you include in this ever-dynamic canon of classical literature? Why?

6. W.E.B. Du Bois says, "The true college will ever have but one goal: not to earn meat but to know the end and aim of the life which meat nourishes." How much thought do you give to the means and ends of your education, especially as it regards outcomes like future salary, job prestige, service to greater society, etc.? Do you think your particular educational setting too easily conflates "means" and "ends" in what they are preparing you for—that is, in seeking "meat" for the sake of "meat" rather than "meat" for the sake of "nourishment"?

7. Discuss: "If reason and the passions are separated, I fear that some students may find radical ideological political projects attractive precisely because they claim to unite the two, becoming a kind of religion."

8. Montaigne says, "You don't die because you're sick, you die because you're alive." And Montás adds that, "You cannot be truly alive except through a vivid apprehension of your death. The tools of a liberal education help us to face these questions around suffering and death." Does our current educational system make enough space for acknowledging the reality of suffering and death? Has your education helped or hindered your ability to find meaning in suffering and death?

9. Discuss Montás's concept of "distractions" as they pertain to disciplining the life of the mind. What are distractions, as opposed to, simply, disturbing aspects of reality? Name some examples that you or others have trouble avoiding. What tools have you found that help you better distance yourself from these distractions?

10. Have you experienced nihilism—the denial of ultimate truth or meaning—in your education?

11. Do you think that reading classics can help build friendship and community across social differences? How?

12. Is a liberal arts education elitist? Idealistic?

13. What are some ways you can continue your own liberal arts education?

REFERENCES

Boccaccio, Giovanni. *The Decameron*. Edited by G. H. McWilliam. London: Penguin Books, 2003.

Bodhi, Bhikkhu, and the Dalai Lama. *In the Buddha's Words: An Anthology of Discourses from the Pali Canon*. Boston: Wisdom Publications, 2005.

Cicero. *De Officiis*. Edited by M. T. Griffin and E. M. Atkins. Cambridge: Cambridge University Press, 1991.

Columbia College. "The Core Curriculum." 2020, at http://www.college.columbia.edu/core/.

Dante. *The Inferno*. Translated by Anthony Esolen. New York: Random House, 2002.

_____. *Purgatory*. Translated by Anthony Esolen. New York: Random House, 2004.

_____. *Paradise*. Translated by Anthony Esolen. New York: Random House, 2007.

Douglass, Frederick. *Narrative of The Life of Frederick Douglass*. Edison: Global Classics, 2020.

Du Bois, W. E. B. *The Souls of Black Folk*. New York: Dover Publications, 2016.

Emerson, Ralph Waldo. "Divinity School Address." Delivered before the Senior Class in Divinity College, Cambridge, July 15, 1838, at archive.vcu.edu/english/engweb/transcendentalism/authors/emerson/essays/dsa.html.

Lewis, C. S. "Learning in War-Time." In *The Weight of Glory*. San Francisco: HarperOne, 1980.

Montaigne, Michel de. *Essays*. New York: Penguin Books, 1958.

Morrison, Toni. *Song of Solomon*. New York: Vintage, 2004.

Murphy, James B. "Why a Core?" *Academic Questions*, September 2006, at www.nas.org/academic-questions/19/3/why_a_core.

Plato. *Plato's Symposium*. Translated by Seth Benardete. Chicago: University of Chicago Press, 2001.

_____. *The Republic of Plato*. Translated by Allan Bloom. New York: Basic Books, 2016.

ADDITIONAL READINGS

Barnett, S. A., David B. Truman, and Daniel Bell. *The Reforming of General Education: The Columbia Experience in Its National Setting*. Abingdon: Routledge, 2017.

Delbanco, Andrew. *College: What It Was, Is, and Should Be*. Revised edition. Princeton: Princeton University Press, 2014.

Harvard University Committee on the Objectives of a General Education in a Free Society. *General Education in a Free Society: Report of the Committee*. Cambridge: Harvard University Press, 1945.

Mooney, Margarita. "Pruning the Mind During a Crisis." *The Hedgehog Review*, April 14, 2020, at hedgehogreview.com/blog/thr/posts/pruning-the-mind-during-a-crisis.

CONCLUSION

Margarita A. Mooney

THIS BOOK is about why the liberal arts tradition is important to living a meaningful life. The dialogical structure of the book is itself a method of educating. This book will have achieved its purpose if it has led you to new insights and encouraged you to renew your commitment to life-long learning. I hope that when you finish this book, you want to ask more questions and dialogue with others about what you have learned from this book.

As I do when teaching, I conclude this book by reviewing areas of agreement across authors, addressing common objections, and making suggestions for continued learning. Although the contributors to this book come from a variety of religious and philosophical perspectives, as well as from different academic disciplines, they all agree that education is a moral endeavor which engages the freedom and uniqueness of both student and teacher. For free human beings who are each unique and called to excellence in different ways, there can be no purely technocratic, scientistic, or entirely skills-based education. All the contributors agree that, although a liberal arts education may look different across contexts, the liberal arts model of education is a necessary component of personal freedom and organic, bottom-up social order. Further, the contributors all agree that a good education requires some tradition, some notion of a core curriculum, and some substantive content. The human mind grows by being exposed to different forms of learning, which includes the scientific method but also literature, music, grammar, rhetoric, and logic.

For free human beings who are each unique and called to excellence in different ways, there can be no purely technocratic, scientistic, or entirely skills-based based education.

In many segments of higher education in the United States, the idea that all knowledge is nothing more than power or that the only objective truth comes from empirical science has become so commonplace as to not be questioned. The agreement among the contributors to this book, that all fields of knowledge ultimately lead to a unified truth, distinguishes a liberal arts education from the other dominant models of education that have shaped American institutions, including models that are purely pragmatic, narrowly scientistic, overly speculative, or exclusively political or social. The heart of a liberal arts education is perhaps best expressed in Augustine's *Confessions*: to seek the truth in a way that is humble yet confident that truth exists.

Although I am persuaded that a liberal arts education contains principles that are universal and therefore applicable across all contexts of education, audiences who have heard me talk about a liberal arts education often still respond with doubts and concerns. One concern is simply that liberal arts education is elitist because it does not place the practical ends of education first, and therefore can only really be for people whose education need not lead to a job. I affirm the dignity of technical work, manual labor, and practical occupations, but do not wish to exclude any human being from the larger sense of educating his or her humanity through literature, philosophy, religion, and also through the theoretical, open-ended aspects of science. A good educational system cannot be simply technical or skills-based or else it risks becoming technocratic and dehumanized. Standards of excellence in education should be for everyone. The greatest ideas that have shaped civilization should not be reserved to only a few in society. There should not be a dichotomy between a liberal arts education and a useful or technical education. On the contrary, only an authentically human education can be useful. In this sense a liberal education is eminently practical in its own right. Yet, a liberal arts education aids a technical education in many ways.

Human development continues across all stages of life. How to educate a person's character and moral behavior remains to be worked out according to his or her particular context—including the age of the learner and the community where the learner resides. The intellectual life and the moral life should shape each other. Without a grounding in a particular moral tradition, however, one many not reach certainty on moral questions simply by reading a particular set of books or sharing certain learning experiences. The idea that reading a certain set of books or acquiring a certain amount of knowledge will automatically lead to good moral character overlooks the importance of the family, religious tradition, and civic life in shaping the moral and ethical commitments requisite for a fulfilling life that contributes to the common good.

Educating people to become members of a particular community in a particular time and place need not mean fearing other times or other cultures. Authority and tradition are inescapable in education, but they need not lead to communities closed off along ethnic or religious lines. American culture is highly individualistic; people will experience many neighborhoods and educational institutions in their lifetime, and much of a person's education will come from his or her own searching, reading, and participation in religious or civic groups. The need for friendship and community in learning is not limited to schooling; it undergirds community life in general, which should include continuing opportunities to learn. Much of what I know, for example, of philosophy, theology, and education, did not come from formal schooling, but from reading on my own and discussing books with mentors or participating in conferences and seminars.

The heart of a liberal arts education is perhaps best expressed in Augustine's Confessions*: to seek the truth in a way that is humble yet confident that truth exists.*

The use of technology is neither always good nor always bad in education; but technology should not be treated as if it were neutral. Our use of technology in learning environments needs to be intentional. Intentional use of technology contributed to the writing of this book, and technology of various kinds can help spread the ideas that form a liberal arts education beyond the boundaries of schools. Yet our brains, and our hearts, need an active, open-ended kind of leisure that technology itself cannot provide.

One need not have a liberal arts education or teach in a school dedicated to the liberal arts to live out these ideals. Anyone can be an exemplary educator who transforms students' lives, because anyone dedicated to the life-long pursuit of knowledge is educating himself or herself and thus has the capacity to educate others. Teaching at any level, in any context, is a vocation. Students as well as their teachers grow intellectually and morally through the art of teaching.

A number of practical suggestions emerge from this book to help you continue your love of learning and teach others the ideas you have learned here.

First, education should start with wonder and curiosity. When have you felt so totally engrossed in learning something that time seemed to stop?

Education is personal. Recall your favorite teacher. What did you learn from that person? Do you long to keep learning about new subjects, to understand how those subjects connect to each other and to practical wisdom? When did you stop or slow your love of learning? Why?

Second, education needs to include the great texts because they are exemplary works. Make a list of a few great books you have always want to read. Why are you waiting? Think of how much time can you dedicate to reading those books—starting today. One new book a year is a great start; more is wonderful if you have the time. Can you start or join a book club, a church group, or some other form of continuing education to give you a sense of community in your journey? How can those communities help you form moral commitments based on what you have learned?

Third, none of us learned everything we wished we had in school. Is there a particular field of knowledge that you can challenge yourself to learn in a different way? Do you know of an exemplar in that field who might suggest to you how to begin to learn?

Fourth, a holistic education should develop our capacity for poetic knowledge. The modern tendency to analyze, measure, and even manipulate reality needs to be balanced by a state of receiving and perceiving reality that opens up to a sacramental way of living—seeing in visible things the invisible grace of God. An openness to transcendence and mystery is necessary to maintain the wonder that gives rise to creativity. What is the place of beauty in your life? Can you integrate beauty into your friendships and daily routines? One helpful practice that I have incorporated into my classes is drawing images which capture the key concepts or central arguments of a book. How might you draw an image or a figure that illustrates what you have learned from reading a great book? Is your relationship with God focused on problems for God to fix? How might you grow in your contemplation of the wonder of creation and the mystery of God's presence in and beyond this world?

Fifth, what does practicing hospitality and developing virtuous friendships look like for you? Are there ways you can incorporate experiences of beauty into your most important friendships and other relationships, including those with whom you work? Who might be your main dialogue partners in the love of learning? What books might you read together, or what beautiful educational experiences might you share?

Finally, what does leisure look like for you? When was the last time you played a game, intentionally practiced humor, or just experienced joy? What might you do to expand your leisure, and how might that leisure deepen your pursuit of knowledge?

In our technocratic, wellness-obsessed society, what we are most missing is the joy, wonder, and child-like ability to marvel at reality. Recovering leisure, friendship, and community is the basis for falling in love with learning again, or for the first time. Since you have made it to the final sentence of the conclusions, now is the time to begin again in your quest for truth!

SHORT GUIDES TO KEY TEXTS IN EDUCATIONAL PHILOSOPHY

Margarita A. Mooney

OVERVIEW

These short guides of the key texts mentioned across this book aim to inform readers of the contents of the texts and share insights to their key ideas regarding their bearing on debates about education. When appropriate, I relate the ideas of one author to other authors in these short guides. I also offer contextual information and acknowledge important critiques.

I have lectured and written on these key texts in educational philosophy in seven full-length classes, as well as in public lectures, webinars and articles aimed at scholars, students, and the general public. These short guides can never replace reading these texts, but the guides aim to present to readers the key ideas that make these texts foundational and worthy of reading. These short guides focus on key themes in each, including: how each author understands the purpose of education and what constitutes a good human life; how each author views teacher-student interactions; and how each author views integrating various fields of knowledge across a curriculum.

The order of the entries corresponds to my own understanding of the relationships between these foundational texts, which may or may not correspond to the date of first publication of each work. Each entry concludes with a brief summary of two or three key points from the pertinent text.

The Idea of a University
JOHN HENRY NEWMAN

DELIVERED AS a series of orations in the mid-nineteenth century, the first few discourses from Saint John Henry Newman's *Idea of a University* consider theology as a branch of knowledge, the relationship of theology to other branches of knowledge, and the unity of knowledge across fields. Later discourses assess how knowledge influences professional occupations and religious duties. This book also has sections dedicated to literature and science, as well as elementary and university education. Reading the entire book may be a challenge to newcomers, but reading even a few discourses is extremely valuable.

Universities certainly should be places for character development, athletic competition, making friends, and living in community. Newman's core message, however, is that we should not lose sight of the unique mission of education: to train the mind to make judgments about reality and to act in accordance with that knowledge. Premises about who we are as human beings and what constitutes the human good undergird all forms of knowledge. The focus on specialized knowledge has limited our ability to acknowledge those premises and to debate which of our premises about foundational questions have the most evidence. The truth of each particular discipline only makes sense if there is an objective truth we are all seeking that stands outside of our particular perspective.

The study of being itself and the study of God (understood, respectively, as metaphysics and theology) are fields of knowledge that are crucial to apprehending the truth in its totality. The absence of theology or metaphysics in many curricula has led to the assumption that only science has a rightful claim to objective truth. Empirical methods and scientific advancements are important, but scientific research simply cannot prove that the only kind of objective knowledge about reality comes from the scientific method. Science cannot replace or refute metaphysics. Science and theology are distinct ways of knowing that need to be integrated, not opposed to each other or reduced one to the other.

For Newman, a liberal arts education is important because a liberal arts education exposes students to various fields that sharpen the mind's ability to perceive reality in a variety of ways. Newman sees the study of subjects like philosophy, ethics, theology, mathematics, and science as necessary to having a well-tuned mind. But as the mind is developed in different ways, no field should be excluded *a priori* from a liberal arts education. The arts—music, painting, literature—also train our mind to apprehend beauty and hence bring us closer to reality. This capacity to perceive reality, not the transmission of knowledge *per se*, forms the purpose of education. Friendship and sharing life in common were so important to the pursuit of truth that Newman founded the Oratory, a community of study and faith.

Newman also claimed that teachers can have a great personal influence on students. The teacher is not simply a conduit of information; the teacher shares knowledge but also communicates an approach to truth, a way of reasoning, and intuiting, and making judgments. Newman himself developed many close friendships with his students, from whom he undoubtedly learned much.

IN BRIEF

- Newman's core message is that we should not lose sight of the unique mission of education: to train the mind to make judgments about reality and to act in accordance with that knowledge. This capacity to perceive reality, not the transmission of knowledge *per se*, forms the purpose of education.
- A liberal arts education is important because it exposes students to various fields that sharpen the mind's ability to perceive reality in a variety of different ways. Science and theology are distinct ways of knowing reality that need to be integrated, not opposed to each other or reduced one to the other.
- Teachers can have a great personal influence on students, not just by transmission of knowledge, but through spiritual friendship and by forming communities of communal worship and learning.

Education at the Crossroads

JACQUES MARITAIN

JACQUES MARITAIN, a Frenchman exiled to the United States because of World War II, offered a profound warning to pragmatic Americans in *Education at the Crossroads* (originally delivered as part of the Terry Lectures at Yale University in 1943). Only a personalist, theistic, and humanist philosophy can provide the basis for education in a free society such as the United States. *Education at the Crossroads* is one of the brilliant Maritain's most accessible works for non-philosophers.

Concerned that debates on education tend to focus on didactic methods, to the detriment of shaping a free human person, Maritain asserts that the end of education is to "to guide man in the evolving dynamism through which he shapes himself as a human person—armed with knowledge, strength of judgment, and moral virtues—while at the same time conveying to him the spiritual heritage of the nation and the civilization in which he is involved, and preserving in this way the century-old achievements of generations" (p. 10).

Maritain, who converted from atheism to Roman Catholicism while studying philosophy in Paris, held to a theistic view of the human person according to which our inner nature has as its final end communion with God, who created us and sustains us. According to Maritain, our rationality points to a transcendent reality beyond direct sensual perception, revealed through our intuitions and our desire for love and truth.

It is because the human person's highest good is communion with God, Maritain argues, that our intellectual nature cannot be entirely reduced to practical action in the world. Part of what educators must do, he contends, is preserve the traditions that represent millennia of wisdom about who we are as human beings, including our desires and final destiny. Apart from a strong tradition that upholds a notion of a transcendent reality, education becomes merely a tool for intervention in the here and now—a tool that can be easily manipulated for evil purposes.

Maritain's thinking on education contrasts with two prominent thinkers who have shaped educational philosophy and policy in the United States: John Dewey, a pragmatist philosopher, and Paulo Freire, a Marxist-influenced philosopher. Maritain commends Dewey for some of his innovative educational methods. He warns, however, that the first mistake in education is to disregard the ends and focus on the means. Although Maritain wrote before Freire, he knew well the impact of Marxist philosophy on education in the Soviet Union and Nazi education in Germany. Maritain feared that Marxist rejection of the idea that humans are a unity of mind, body, and soul would force education to serve a political project rather than the promotion of human freedom.

At the crux of Maritain's disagreement with Dewey and Freire is the question of the nature of the human person. For both Dewey and Freire, the human intellect is essentially a tool for action in the world—whether that be problem-solving action (Dewey) or fighting for revolutionary liberation (Freire). Maritain does not disregard the practical ends of education. But he argues that we best achieve these ends by keeping in mind that we are persons, body and soul—beings with an interior life that cannot be reduced to one or another social role.

In Chapter 2, Maritain argues that the teacher brings her own subjectivity, her whole self, into the classroom, and must seek to constantly activate the inner dynamism of the student, which is the true means and end of education. Chapter 3 builds on Newman's insights about the nature of knowledge and the structure of the curriculum at the elementary and high school levels as well as that of the university. Maritain argues that a liberal arts education, starting in elementary school and continuing through university, aims at forming intellectual virtues in students. Specialization has its place in education, but liberal education prepares the student both for future work and for leisure. Maritain proposes a college curriculum that would include mathematics, poetry, natural sciences, and fine arts, as well as the foundations of wisdom from philosophy and theology.

In Chapter 4, Maritain ponders how education, as he conceives it, cannot take place in the classroom alone. Our moral nature, our capacity to love, and our desires for leisure and beauty are gifts of our creator that can only be fulfilled and developed through their integration with family, church, and educational institutions. He concludes by warning that the downstream impact of pragmatist, Marxist, or any atheist or materialist philosophy that ignores the contemplative dimension of our humanity is that culture and education will end in a "a stony positivist or technocratic denial of the objective value of any spiritual need" (p. 115).

IN BRIEF

- Apart from a strong tradition that upholds a notion of a transcendent reality and the interior life of the human person, education could become merely a tool for intervention in the here and now—a tool that can be easily manipulated for evil purposes.
- The teacher brings her own subjectivity, her whole self, into the classroom, and must seek to constantly activate the inner dynamism of the student, which is the true means and end of education.
- Specialization has its place in education, but youth must be exposed to a liberal education for the future work and leisure. A college curriculum should include mathematics, poetry, natural sciences, and fine arts, as well as the foundations of wisdom from philosophy and theology.
- Education goes beyond school, as our moral nature, our capacity to love, and our desires for leisure and beauty are gifts that can only be fulfilled and developed through their integration with family, church, and educational institutions.

"My Pedagogic Creed" and *Democracy and Education*

JOHN DEWEY

EVEN IF the explicit curriculum of Americans schools is more often shaped by standardized tests than the work of a philosopher, educators in the United States continue to be initiated into a philosophy of education inspired by the pragmatist John Dewey.

Dewey, born in Vermont in 1859, was trained at Johns Hopkins University and began his teaching career at the University of Michigan before becoming a faculty member at the newly formed University of Chicago. At Chicago, he was the founder of a laboratory school that inspired American education moving forward.

Although he wrote on topics related to epistemology, science, and art, Dewey is best known for his works on education. His 1897 article "My Pedagogic Creed" is a succinct summary of his educational philosophy, introducing readers to a philosophy of education grounded in the social formation of the student. For Dewey, all education is a social process whereby the student is initiated into the practices of a specific society. This education is not about passing on information but instead capacitating the powers of the student to respond to the various situations that he or she will face as a member of a social unit. Dewey writes, "I believe that the only true education comes through the stimulation of the child's powers by the demands of the social situations in which he finds himself." The education of the child creates an environment whereby those natural capacities of the child may be exercised. The purpose of the school is to establish a simplified environment in which the child participates in projects related to the living, social world of that child. Readers will be familiar with Dewey's approach to education if they have ever spent time in a preschool or kindergarten classroom.

For Dewey, education has no other end than the educational process itself. Subject matter is important insofar as it fosters the living capacities of the child. But, in contrast to Newman and Maritain, Dewey rejects the disciplines of a typical liberal arts curriculum, since such an education would force the student to consider questions that might not emerge from something he or she has experienced in the world. As he writes in "My Pedagogic Creed," "I believe that to set up any end out of education, as furnishing its goal and standard, is to deprive the educational process of much of its meaning and tends to make us rely upon false and external stimuli in dealing with the child."

Dewey eventually did argue for an end to an education that was based in political life. In later works, such as *Democracy and Education* (1916), Dewey argues for a *telos* of education founded in democracy. Democracy, for Dewey, is more than a system of governance resting upon popular opinion. Rather, democracy is a certain capaciousness of thought, a non-dogmatic approach to the world grounded in a social conversation around the pursuit of "continuous readjustment through meeting the new situations produced by varied intercourse" (p. 100). The educational process must form the child to participate in this social process of continued readjustment to the situations of the day. Education should therefore initiate the child into a reflective mode of experience, one in which the child learns to recognize a problem and to pursue it, to develop a hypothesis, to conduct an experiment whereby one comes to test one's hypothesis, to adjust this hypothesis based on the experiment, and to make a judgment about a potential plan of action in light of this hypothesis. Subject matter in education remains important insofar as it is essential in providing an environment whereby the student may pursue this inquiry. This quest for democratic capaciousness of thought is for Dewey the dawning rays of the kingdom of God, a common faith in American democracy in which human beings may grow ever closer to their potential as infinite knowers and prudent actors in the world.

In *Education at the Crossroads,* Maritain recognizes explicitly the contributions made to education by John Dewey, especially his attention to the social context of education. Like Dewey, Maritain also rejects an educational rigidity where young students are lined up in classrooms, lectured for hours, and then told to reproduce that material on an exam. But Maritain is clear that Dewey's approach to education brackets out the question of truth in the educational act. Thought, for Dewey, becomes nothing more than a kind of instrumental activity moving toward action within a society. An integral education, for Maritain, must not let the insights of educational figures like Dewey lead us away from the spiritual nature of knowing and the recognition of an interior freedom within the human person that transcends the social order.

IN BRIEF

- For Dewey, all education is a social process whereby the student is initiated into the practices of a specific society. The purpose of the school is to establish a simplified environment in which the child participates in projects related to the living, social world of that child.
- Education should initiate the child into a reflective mode of experience, one in which the child learns to recognize a problem and to pursue it, to develop a hypothesis, to conduct an experiment whereby one comes to test one's hypothesis, to adjust this hypothesis based on the experiment, and to make a judgment about a potential plan of action in light of this hypothesis.

> * Dewey believed that education should further a common faith in American democracy, which he believed would help students grow ever closer to their potential as infinite knowers and prudent actors in the world. Although he believed in a God who is present through practical action in the world, he did not believe in truth that emanates from a transcendent, supernatural order, such as metaphysics or theology.

Pedagogy of the Oppressed
PAULO FREIRE

PUBLISHED IN 1968, Paulo Freire's book *Pedagogy of the Oppressed* remains a perennial bestseller and is widely read in teacher training programs. Freire begins by describing the problems of dehumanization caused by poverty. Part of the reason for this book's enduring influence is undoubtedly that, in Chapter 2, Freire colorfully draws on his work in educating illiterate peasants in Brazil to critique what he calls the banking model of education, where education is narrowly understood as the rote memorization of abstract knowledge that has no relationship to one's personal experience. Freire uses lively language in asserting that the banking model of education turns students into "containers" or "receptacles"; the teacher deposits information and the students "patiently receive, memorize, and repeat" (p. 72). Freire contrast those methods to his view of education as consciousness-raising through dialogue that leads to practical action in the world.

Beyond merely describing the banking model, Freire analyzes how the banking model of education emerges from an oppressive social and political system linked to capitalism. Making students passive is not an accident, according to Freire; capitalist education is designed to dehumanize people so they do not resist their oppression.

Freire proposes a problem-solving model of education that would awaken people's consciousness about their social and political situation and lead them to transform their context. Education that humanizes, according to Freire, would link reflection and action. In his model, abstract learning is replaced by critical thinking. Critical thinking leads to concrete action. Dehumanization is replaced by consciousness-raising. In this practice of education as liberation, the power dynamic between student and teacher should disappear, and a dynamic of fellowship and dialogue that produces solidarity should emerge. In Chapter 3, Freire elaborates this method of dialogue.

Although it may seem as if Freire is just presenting a model of education, his educational method is based on a particular understanding of history—a Marxist reading of history. In Chapter 4, he elaborates on the relationship between education and revolutionary action to overthrow oppression and achieve a new cultural synthesis. He draws on the writings and actions of Lenin, Guevara, Mao, Althusser, and other revolutionary thinkers and actors to propose a cultural synthesis through education that needs to undergird revolutionary change to overthrow capitalism.

Is Freire's end goal merely a new model of education? Or is his model of education a means to a true Marxist revolution in which peasants, not just a bourgeois vanguard, take the reins of their place in history, end capitalism, and change culture?

Freire's model works towards its desired end *if* and *when* teachers pass on their Marxist philosophy to students. Yet Marx explicitly denied a transcendent dimension to reality. Freire's ultimate concern is that students reject their passivity and embrace their power to become a revolutionary. But that approach to education leaves out the transcendent, contemplative dimensions of human experience.

Another limitation of Freire's approach is that he collapses truth-seeking and consciousness-raising about the oppressive structures of capitalism. Freire hardly addresses how we should educate people to think about perennial human questions regarding right and wrong, good and evil. It is unclear whether any and all revolutionary action to overthrow capitalism, including violent action, is morally justified.

Unless one has a theory of human development and the human good, the practical application of Freire's many insights about teaching methods remain unfeasible. Freire does not seem to place authority in a tradition of knowledge nor does he credit teachers with wisdom about perennial human questions. It is also unclear how a teacher would respect a student's right to disagree with what the teacher sees as the correct problem to pose. Although dialogue and awareness of history are important, it does not follow that the poor and oppressed are uninterested in truth-seeking beyond revolutionary action to overthrow oppression.

Although Freire wants people to change their way of thinking or acting, only personal experience, not something that transcends the self, is offered as a guide. Freire lacks an objective way to judge, integrate, accept or reject certain aspects of our experiences. To become aware of injustices and act to change them requires an alternative framework of human dignity and a unity of life, which, as Maritain, Giussani, and Newman make clear, is made possible by the gift of life and love that comes from a transcendent God—but this is an aspect of reality that Freire neglects to acknowledge.

A good education introduces students to different ways of understanding ultimate reality and respects their freedom to evaluate those interpretive frameworks. An activist education that is deaf to contemplation too often leads to disorderly actions with limited impact. Students too easily can slide into despair or existential nihilism—the idea that the world is devoid of meaning or that the universe is chaotic—because they are unable to convince or compel others to follow their paths or change the world as they hoped.

IN BRIEF

- Freire proposes a problem-solving model of education that would awaken people's consciousness about their social and political situation and lead them to transform their context.
- In this practice of education as liberation, the power dynamic between student and teacher should disappear, and a dynamic of fellowship and dialogue that produces solidarity should emerge.
- Freire draws on the writings and actions of Lenin, Guevara, Mao, Althusser, and other revolutionary thinkers and actors to propose a cultural synthesis through education that seeks to undergird revolutionary change and overthrow capitalism.
- Freire's approach collapses truth-seeking into nothing more than consciousness-raising about the oppressive structures of capitalism. He does not explicitly acknowledge a transcendent dimension to the human person; as such, all knowledge is oriented toward liberation through revolutionary action in the world.

The Risk of Education
LUIGI GIUSSANI

BORN IN 1922, Luigi Giussani was an Italian Catholic priest and founder of the movement Communion and Liberation. He was also a scholar and teacher who understood the crisis of modernity. He developed an educational method aimed at integrating the transcendent dimension of the human person into learning, friendship, family, and community grounded in a shared experience of faith in Jesus.

The Risk of Education is one of his shortest books. It distills the key elements of his educational method, which emanates from an integrated vision of the human person as a unity of mind, body, and soul, as expounded by Newman and Maritain (and by Giussani himself in his many other writings, including *The Religious Sense*).

Giussani's approach includes examining the original meaning of words that are sometimes left out of education, including reason, tradition, and authority. For example, reason is a term which is often reduced to the scientific method, which consists of running experiments and collecting empirical observations. For Giussani, following a long tradition of Greek and Christian thinking, reason is always open to the infinite. One characteristic of being human is that we ponder the unseen; we come to know the world through science and through signs (a point he develops in *The Religious Sense*).

The end of education, per Giussani, is coming to know ourselves in personal relation to God, who created us for eternal communion with him. Knowing God is central to knowing how to live and act in this world, but, because humans have a soul that transcends this world, knowing how to act in this world is not the only thing we need to know.

For Giussani, a dialogue between student and teacher or among students does not start from nowhere. Nor can dialogue lead to skepticism about truth. For Giussani, the teacher does not only pose problems in the world that need to be solved. In dialogue with students, critique and provocation are not aimed at tearing down a framework just for the sake of it. The teacher has a definite responsibility to share with students an interpretive framework that is necessary in order for one to go from personal experience to the kinds of moral judgments that influence actions. This interpretive framework, this starting point for learning and for experience, is tradition.

Although dialogue is crucial to Giussani's method, teachers also bring authority into the classroom. But teachers are most effective when they can connect what they teach to their own experience; if this experience, upon rational examination, is deemed to be true by the student, it will lead the student to make a commitment to a particular tradition and to a particular community that embodies that tradition.

Allowing students to engage in this provocation is why Giussani calls his educational method a risk. Teachers must love the freedom of their students as they engage in this educational process of verifying a tradition, and students must love the embodied authority—a person or a living tradition like the church—that breaks open (but does not break down) their way of reasoning to make it consistent with a way of living.

Developing his methodology precisely in response to Marxist student movements across Europe that implicitly denied the transcendent dimension of the human person, Giussani warned that when educational systems embrace a notion of collective liberation, but reject personal liberation through a relationship with God, it becomes all too easy to turn the collective into another kind of god that subjugates the value of the individual to one or another social goal. True solidarity is based on a respect for the mystery of each person's subjectivity.

Although Giussani was a teacher of theology, his approach is applicable to all forms of knowledge because all forms of knowledge—including science—are supposed to lead to encounters with a shared transcendent reality. Giussani's method embraces the human longing to not simply solve problems but to arrive at certainty about truth. Giussani lays out a method of dialogue in the search for truth that respects the freedom and mystery of each person.

IN BRIEF

- Following a long tradition of Greek and Christian thinking, Giussani sees our reason as always open to the infinite. One characteristic of being human is that we ponder the unseen; we come to know the world through science and through signs (a point he develops in *The Religious Sense*).
- The teacher has a responsibility to share with students an interpretive framework for moving from personal experience to the kinds of moral judgments that influence actions.
- This interpretive framework, this starting point for learning, is tradition. Tradition is a starting point, or a testing ground, for personal experience.
- Giussani calls his educational method a risk because it allows students to engage in this provocation and to examine of tradition. Giussani's dialogical method aims to lead students to the truth but also respects the mystery and freedom of each person.

The Religious Sense
LUIGI GIUSSANI

The Religious Sense is likely Luigi Giussani's most widely read book. Chapters 11-13 are helpful to further understand his educational philosophy.

Chapter 11, "The Experience of the Sign," builds on Saint Augustine to posit that human beings intrinsically desire to know the truth. As Augustine himself learned, only an ultimate truth can provide an integrative framework for partial truths. Giussani also elaborates the idea of reality as a sign, which is important to understand his emphasis on human existence being fulfilled by something that is beyond us, something to which we are attracted through beauty and love. He concludes this chapter by discussing his definition of reason as "the need for an adequate, total explanation of existence" (p. 116), including the symbolic dimension of reality.

Chapter 12, a brief chapter called "The Adventure of Interpretation," further explains why humans long to encounter the transcendent in their search for truth. The fact that some learned persons in science, literature, and philosophy have been led to God by their scientific knowledge, whereas others reject God, is evidence that we have freedom in how we use our reason. Giussani warns against the myopia of positivism, which tells us to that know something we should reduce it to its smallest elements. Instead, Giussani calls for us to approach reality—including science—as a sign which needs to be unveiled, an approach which requires stepping back, paying close attention, and cultivating a sense of wonder. His method of approaching reality, Giussani maintains, comes closer to the geniuses of science like Albert Einstein than the positivist approach to knowledge, which constitutes and unexamined assumption in many approaches to reality.

Chapter 13, "An Education in Freedom," draws out the implications for human freedom that stem from seeing the symbolic dimension of reality, which in turn requires a contemplative aspect of our reason. For Giussani, education begins with paying attention, learning how to ask questions, and being willing to take the risk to take practical steps as well as make moral commitments based on what we learn. Our responsibility for ourselves and for others cannot be fulfilled without risking our freedom and making commitments.

IN BRIEF

- Giussani describes how human existence is fulfilled by something that is beyond us, to which we are attracted through beauty and love. He defines reason as "the need for an adequate, total explanation of existence" (p. 116), including the symbolic dimension of reality.
- Giussani warns against the use of reason as merely a method of reducing something to its smallest elements. Instead, he calls for us to approach reality as a sign whose meaning needs to be unveiled.
- Education for Giussani requires paying attention, learning how to ask questions, and being willing to take the risk to make concrete steps as well as moral commitments based on the fruits of our education.

Leisure: The Basis of Culture
JOSEF PIEPER

THE PURSUIT of knowledge, the acquisition of some amount of content, is crucial to an education. In his book *Leisure: The Basis of Culture,* the German philosopher Josef Pieper (1904–1997) poses a challenging question: "Is knowledge only acquired through arduous mental labor?"

Similar to Giussani, Pieper writes: "The essence of knowledge does not consist in the effort for which it calls, but in grasping existing things and in unveiling reality. Moreover, just as the highest form of virtue knows nothing of 'difficulty,' so too the highest form of knowledge comes to man like a gift—the sudden illumination, a stroke of genius, true contemplation; it comes effortlessly, and without trouble" (p. 34).

By stripping education of its contemplative dimension, much of how we learn has become so arduous that we lack the wonder and creativity brings us to new heights. All of our lives have come the realm of what Pieper calls "total work."

Pieper's important contribution in this short but dense book is to return to a classical understanding of leisure that is distinct from laziness. Leisure is not *acedia,* the vice which Pieper defines as sadness overwhelming man. Pieper writes that leisure is not entertainment; leisure is a condition for true education to occur. Leisure "is a mental and spiritual attitude... It is, in the first place, an attitude of mind, a condition of the soul" (p. 46). Thus, for Pieper, true education does not end in dominating the world with total work but is a consistent return to a sense of wonder that increases our desire to know more about the world.

IN BRIEF

- Stripping education of its contemplative dimension results in our learning becoming so arduous that we lack the wonder and creativity that brings us to new heights.
- Leisure is a condition for true education to occur because a true education does not end in dominating the world with total work but always returns to a sense of wonder that increases our desire to know more about the world.

The Love of Learning and the Desire for God

JEAN LECLERCQ

THE LOVE OF LEARNING and the Desire for God is a study of monastic culture written by a Benedictine monk, Jean Leclercq, who was born in France in 1911. In addition to the general introduction on learning and spirituality in a monastic context, Chapter 7, entitled "Liberal Studies," helps put into context how monks aimed for a humanistic synthesis of all knowledge. Leclercq calls this integral humanism, a term also used by Maritain in his work on the common good.

In the Benedictine tradition, which dates back to the fifth century, monks study the Church Fathers and Scripture, as well as classical texts from non-Christian authors like Virgil, simply because these texts are beautiful. Benedictines believe that every written work which is good or beautiful comes from the hand of God, even if its author was not a Christian.

Monks made every effort to find a good intention in these works—in marked distinction to contemporary efforts to deconstruct and debunk classical texts. Reflecting back on Benedictine monks in the *scriptorium* who pondered classical texts, Leclercq explains, "At times they drew moral lessons from these authors, but they were not, thanks be to God, reduced to looking to them for that. Their desire was for the joys of the spirit, and they neglected none that these authors had to offer. So if they transcribed classical texts it is simply because they loved them" (p. 134).

Integral humanism acknowledges that studying the world does not equate to anthropocentrism, wherein the human person is the center of reality. We can perceive and study reality through direct observation. But there is also a world we do not see directly—we perceive that reality through the beauty of the world that constitutes a sign of another reality.

An integral humanist approach to learning celebrates discoveries about nature and our work in the world, but also acknowledges human limits and our dependence on a creator. The more knowledge we have, the more our desire for the infinite is awakened, and therefore the more we can love ourselves, others, and our creator.

Leclercq's book demonstrates that a monastic approach to education does not lead to communities wholly set apart from the world. An education should transmit one's own tradition while appreciating insights on truth from other traditions and practicing hospitality, an openness to learning from others.

IN BRIEF

- In a Benedictine approach to liberal studies, everything that is good or beautiful is seen as coming from the hand of God.
- An integral humanist approach to learning celebrates discoveries about nature and human work in the world. The more knowledge we have, the more our desires grow to love ourselves, love others, and love our creator.

- A monastic approach to education does not have to mean separation from the world. An education should transmit one's own tradition while appreciating insights on truth from other traditions and practicing hospitality, an openness to learning from others.

GUIDE FOR DISCUSSION GROUPS

MARGARITA A. MOONEY

WHY HAVE YOU READ THIS BOOK? WHY READ THIS BOOK WITH OTHERS, MAYBE EVEN IN A GROUP?

IF YOU are wondering whether to invest your time in this book, I encourage you to ask yourself the following questions: What did you like most about your education? What did you like the least? Do you wish you had more knowledge of one kind or another? Do you wish you understood better how to connect knowledge to practical wisdom for life?

Or, if you are reading this guide after you have reached the end of the book: What led you to read it? What were the questions or concerns that brought you to invest your time in reading it? How has the book helped you cultivate a greater commitment to ideas, practices, and people? What can you do to take what you have learned from the book back to your own environment?

Whether you are reading this guide for discussion groups before or after you read the book, I encourage you to think about giving the book to at least one other person and asking him or her to read it with you and discuss it. Why? We learn most deeply when learning alongside others, sharing what we learn, and listening to what they have learned. As a teacher, I am blessed to do this every day—my job is to bring great ideas to communities of learners and guide them through these ideas so that they might apply them in their own lives.

I have been blessed to be a professor for more than fifteen years, teaching hundreds of students from college freshmen to advanced doctoral students; leading seminars for other scholars to introduce them to new texts and ideas; running countless discussion groups of varying sizes, whether church groups or student groups; and and I have participated in many more discussion groups and seminars myself. All of these experiences as a teacher and life-long learner have helped me assemble this guide for reading this book in a group.

WAYS TO READ THE BOOK

DEPENDING ON your background or purpose, you can read the book over a variety of different lengths of time. For any of these formats discussed below, I recommend you make use of the videos that were the original dialogues, or the video clips. Videos are dynamic: they grab our attention and open up questions. The written text allows our minds to slow down, ponder certain points deeply, and look back at the arc of a dialogue with a beginning, a middle, and an end.

These chapters grew out of a series of dialogues—they were originally spoken out loud. I recommend reading out loud from the text regardless of which format you use. Naturally, when discussing more than one chapter in a session, one has less time to read the entire chapter out loud. I recommend, however, highlighting key sections, quotes, or entire paragraphs, and reading them out loud together. We learn with our minds and our ears; reading and listening reinforce each other.

You may also choose from the list of references at the end of each chapter to do additional reading, and/or read sections of the Short Guides to Key Texts in Educational Philosophy, or chapters from those sources.

Here are some suggestions for various formats for a discussion group on this text.

1. Read one chapter at a time, adding the introduction and conclusion to the first and last weeks, respectively. This format would work well to read the chapters out loud together and discuss.

2. Read two chapters at a time over a four-week period, adding the introduction to Chapters 1 and 2 in Week 1 and the conclusion to Chapter 7 in Week 4. In this format, reading should be done in advance, but I encourage you to pick certain sections to read out loud.

3. You could set aside an entire day and split the chapters into 4 sessions, following the same breakdown as Suggestion 2.

4. This book can also be taught as part of a longer course on education or philosophy. Each chapter can be assigned along with some primary readings from the books in the Short Guides and/or some of the additional readings listed in the references of each chapter. For this model, I have found it helpful to combine additional readings from the denser philosophical texts with some of the more contemporary pieces that get at current debates and challenges in education.

WHOM TO GATHER?

ALTHOUGH THIS book is aimed at anyone with a life-long interest in learning, it could be fruitful for groups to read this book together who can then apply the insights to their particular circumstances. Some particular groups of people who might benefit from reading this book together include:

- Educators (teachers at any level from K–12 or higher education; anyone who works in student life, like high school guidance counselors or deans in higher education).
- Policymakers (legislators and administrators).
- Students.
- Parents.
- Life-long learners.
- Families.

The first meeting of a discussion group is crucial. Ask everyone to introduce themselves, say what brought them to the group, and what they hope to get out of it.

How big should the group be? As an educator, I have seen time and again that in groups larger than twelve, in-depth discussion becomes harder. Maybe this is the reason Jesus had twelve and only twelve disciples. Groups with six to eight people work well because everyone has a chance to talk, and you will hear a variety of perspectives. But groups of two, three, and four are also great. If you are fortunate to have more than twelve people interested in reading this book, I would recommend finding ways to get people to actively engage with each other about the reading, such as breaking down into sections of three or four people, for part of the time, and having one person per section report back to the main group.

TIME

HOW SHOULD the time in a discussion group be allocated?

If you have two hours, you may wish to discuss the reading over a meal. Take thirty or, at most, forty-five minutes to gather, eat, converse, and then start the discussion. Or you can reverse the order, having the formal discussion first and then continuing to talk over a meal.

If you have less time, meet for at least one hour or preferably an hour and a half. Provision of snacks and water, coffee, and tea is always pleasant. But by all means do not feel pressured to be Martha the anxious hostess: people can bring their own snacks and water.

BASIC EXPECTATIONS

TIMELINESS, PRAYER, *and respect.* Try to start on time and end on time. Start the group with prayer if you feel comfortable. If everyone in the group does not identify as a person with a faith tradition, or the same faith is not shared, people can take turns starting the group off in a way that makes them feel comfortable. Each member could share his or her own religious tradition, or some such manner of establishing intentions when entering into a learning setting. Many people will have experiences that allow them to lead the group in this way; those who do not will learn from others. Never force anyone to lead in this way if they feel uncomfortable; rarely, or more likely never, have I seen anyone opposed to a group starting off this way even if they do not share the opening prayers or thoughts. This is part and parcel of respecting each person's starting-point.

Speak openly. Be willing to challenge others and be challenged yourself. Be civil, as that will help in our common purpose of getting to the truth together. Participate in discussions. Everyone has something to share about every reading. One tip for the denser readings is to focus on a few paragraphs or concepts that you would like to discuss more in depth during class discussions. Through discussions of these texts with friends and colleagues your comprehension of the texts will continue to progress.

Be careful not to make assumptions about others. People come from varying backgrounds and fields of knowledge. When bringing in personal experiences or knowledge from your own field to seminar discussions, try to connect them to the shared content of the seminar so that it contributes to understanding the big questions guiding our shared inquiry.

Practice the intellectual and personal virtues that will support discussions, such as timeliness in arriving and generosity and forbearance with others.

DISCUSSION GROUP ROLES

ONE PERSON need not do everything in a discussion group. Here are some responsibilities for a successful discussion group that can be divided up across various people. The roles in a discussion group need not be this formal, but having some roles set in advance can help. Especially for those who have not been in a classroom or been in a discussion group in a while, having an assigned role can help active engagement.

Discussion Leader. In my experience, groups that have a discussion leader or facilitator work the best. The discussion leader is supposed to guide the group. At a minimum, the discussion leader gets the discussion going by bringing out a few key points or questions; keeps the discussion going if it slows down; and can bring in additional research about each particular chapter (provided those new insights are kept accessible to those who have not done additional reading). In general, the kinds of questions that can be asked are (1) clarification; (2) inspiration; (3) application; and (4) additional questions beyond the scope of the reading.

If your group has a particularly knowledgeable discussion leader, that person can take on a bigger role to provide insights and guidance that deepen the common understanding of the text. Those insights can come from one's own experience with the topic and/or from some additional reading or previous knowledge. Be careful not to let the guidance you give—whether that be from personal experience or outside knowledge—take over and become a lecture. Keep your introductory comments, if you make them, to five or ten minutes at the absolute most. If you happen to be an expert on a topic being covered, do not expect that you can lecture and get others to engage deeply with a text they have not read, especially when it is something complex. You can introduce one or two concepts or quotes from outside reading, but not much more.

Organizer. Sets the dates of meetings, finds the place to meet, picks the chapters to read at each meeting.

Note-Taker. Records the important points and distributes them to the group after each session.

Participants. Every group member needs to commit time and energy to do the reading in advance, reflect on the reading, and ask questions. Listen to others. Listen deeply to what is stirring in your own heart and share your insights. Prepare. Complete the reading in advance (or listen attentively if your group is reading the text out loud together) and prepare yourself to share your thoughts. Undoubtedly, some of the ideas are challenging. Do not hesitate to say which ideas you found most difficult and ask for clarification.

WHERE TO MEET

DISCUSSION GROUPS can be run anywhere, really—whether at someone's home, in a coffee shop, or online. Face to face is normally preferable, but online groups are great for connecting people across distances.

GUEST SPEAKERS

ESPECIALLY FOR church groups and classes, inviting guests to the group can be beneficial. People who are experts are often busy, but people also generally like to speak about ideas they are passionate about. Having guest speakers is not necessary for a group to be successful, but it is absolutely worth trying. If you invite a guest speaker, be clear to them what you expect them to do, whether it be to give a lecture, share their experiences, or simply read the text along with your group.

WHAT TO DO WHEN THE GROUP CONCLUDES

THIS BOOK is supposed to change how you live. I encourage you to make concrete resolutions to further your own education. Don't let this just be another book you read—take action. Can you create your own wish list of lifetime reading and make a plan to read a certain number of books a year? Does your group want to ask each member to define a project you want to work on and hold each other accountable? For teachers at any level, your project could be a new course, a new syllabus, or an orientation program for your students. If the group was a success, does the group want to pick a new book to read together?

HOW DISCUSSION GROUPS GO WRONG AND WHAT TO DO

SOMETIMES DISCUSSION groups can go wrong. If they do, you can always start off a session explaining the goals and format again. If you absolutely have to, talk privately to someone who dominates the group discussion or is impolite to others when they participate. Some people rarely participate, and it may be important to ask them if they have time to do the reading or are just shy. People who are shy often prefer to have a role, or an assigned time to participate, and do not like to be called on. They might be great listeners and note-takers.

Some people talk out loud to discover a point they wish to make. This can be hard for others in the group who are unable to follow their comments or see how they are related to the reading. Giving a few minutes at the start to write down insights and questions, and gently interrupting to ask people to relate what they are saying back to the text, can help.

Do not be afraid of having your ideas challenged or of challenging someone else's ideas. Remember also to leave room to understand or contextualize someone's comment. Questions such as, "Can you say more about that?" or "Can you give an example of that?" may help the speaker to explain their reasoning without feeling unduly challenged.

About the Scala Foundation

Scala is a movement of students and educators who are committed to the transformational, holistic tradition of liberal arts education. Liberal arts education is gained through schooling and also in families, churches, and any place where people learn to love truth and experience beauty. Inspired by a tradition of education open to transcendence, Scala's programs create an environment that models a view of leisure, beauty, friendship as intrinsic human goods best fulfilled in community.

Scan to visit SCALAFOUNDATION.ORG

CLUNY MEDIA

Designed by Fiona Cecile Clarke, the Cluny Media *logo depicts a monk at work in the scriptorium, with a cat sitting at his feet.*

The monk represents our mission to emulate the invaluable contributions of the monks of Cluny in preserving the libraries of the West, our strivings to know and love the truth.

The cat at the monk's feet is Pangur Bán, from the eponymous Irish poem of the 9th century. The anonymous poet compares his scholarly pursuit of truth with the cat's happy hunting of mice. The depiction of Pangur Bán is an homage to the work of the monks of Irish monasteries and a sign of the joy we at Cluny take in our trade.

"Messe ocus Pangur Bán,
cechtar nathar fria saindan:
bíth a menmasam fri seilgg,
mu memna céin im saincheirdd."

Made in the USA
Middletown, DE
25 September 2022

11073879R00136